Escaping Death

Escaping Death

THE FIGHT AGAINST L.I.F.E.

JEFF WYLIE

This is a work of fiction. Names, characters, places, and incidents either are the product of the author's imagination or are used fictitiously, and any resemblance to actual persons, living or dead, business establishments, events, countries or locales is entirely coincidental.

All Rights Reserved
Copyright © 2022 by The Smith Group

No part of this book may be reproduced or transmitted, downloaded, distributed, reverse engineered, or stored in or introduced into any information storage and retrieval system, in any form or by any means, including photocopying and recording, whether electronic or mechanical, now known or hereinafter invented without permission in writing from the publisher.

ISBN: 978-1-64133-753-3
eISBN: 978-1-64133-754-0

Brilliant Books Literary
137 Forest Park Lane Thomasville
North Carolina 27360 USA

As Fate Would Have It

"Daddy, back up, way far, okay!" shouted Gain, who was four and a half years old. The two were in the backyard playing catch with the football. Gain had been practicing how to throw the ball and was anxious to show how much he had improved. The fact is, Gain had been watching his father and was ... well, as most boys are at his age, absolutely amazed. His father, Allen Watson, was extremely athletic and very intelligent, and at the same time, he was very much into his son.

At 6 feet 6 inches tall, 235 pounds, coming out of high school, Allen was destined to be one of the best; if not the best quarterback professional football had ever seen. From the time he took his first snap in a regulation game, at the age of 10, until his last snap taken as a senior, during the final seconds of the state championship game, Allen had only been sacked once; his first snap. From then on, no one could get to him. This was not because he always had a "lock-down" offensive line. Simply put, Allen was gifted.

While he did take a few hits in his football career, he was always able to throw the pass he wanted, with great accuracy, before the defenders could bring him down. No one had more "full ride" offers to more colleges than Allen did. And that final state championship game … his team won in dramatic fashion. It was the last play of the game and his team was down by 5 points. Allen dropped back to pass the ball, but everyone was covered, and as the rush became heavy, he began to scramble and dodge the would-be tacklers until at last he saw his main receiver, wide open. Allen launched the ball. It traveled for 60 yards and was caught in the endzone for the game winning touchdown! The crowd was roaring. Allen's teammates were shouting and leaping, and Allen … He was hurt … badly. Three defenders hit him almost simutaniously, just as the ball left his hand. The three of them stood over him praying.

It would be three days before Allen awoke to realize what had happened on that night. He was ecstatic about the news that his team won the championship, but more than just a victory happened. In addition to suffering a concussion that put him in a mild coma, Allen shattered his left knee cap, and destroyed the tendons in the shoulder of his throwing arm. His life as a football player was over. It has been said that we are all in control of our own destinies. Fate, however is not impressed by our decisions, whether big or small, good or bad it changes for no being, and yields only to the motions of its creator.

"Well, how far do you want me to go?" Gain's father replied. Then Gain said with a confident voice, "I'm going to turn around and start counting to ten. When I start counting, you can start backing up till I get to ten." Gain's father knew that if he had backed up at a normal pace, he would have gotten too far away. So he backed up slowly with baby steps, and just as he had hoped, he was still fairly close after Gain finished counting. But when Gain turned around and saw that his father was so close, he wasn't satisfied with the distance. He wanted his father to see that he could throw the ball very far. So he plainly told his father, "Back up until I say stop." Gain's father chuckled and said as he began to back up, "Okay, son, tell me when to stop." "I will," said Gain. So Gain's father began to back up, and as he did, Gain began to mimic some of his dad's moves; pretending to dodge defenders. Allen stopped and said "Where did you learn how to do that?" "From you daddy," answered Gain. "You let me watch your videos all the time." "Ah yeah," Allen said to himself, "I did not know he was paying much attention." "I've been practicing daddy … a lot," said Gain. "Look!" Gain rocked back and threw the ball as hard as he could so that the ball went over his father's head and landed about 20 yards away.

Allen was pleasantly shocked at the amount of talent his son possessed, but before he could make a comment, something horrible happened. From the woods nearby, a huge, rabid dog had made its way into their back yard. He came from the woods nearby. The Watson's back yard was quite sizeable. The lawn, which was fenced only in the back to give separation from the wooded area of their neighborhood, was about an acre. On the other side of the fence was a grassy area and about 50 yards from the fence was the woods.

It did not take long after leaving the woods before the dog had climbed the fence, and was running toward Gain; barking and growling, about to attack. The dog was nearly three times Gain's size, so he fell to the ground curled up into a ball, and covered his head with his arms and hands. At the very moment that Gain fell, Allen charged the dog as if he had brand new knees, dove, and tackled him. The dog, redirecting his rage toward Allen, created a scuffle. As the two wrestled, Gain's father yelled, "Run, Gain! Go inside the house!" Gain listened to his father, but as he was running, he looked back and saw that the dog was leaving, headed back toward the woods. As Gain watched the dog climb over to the other side of the fence, he quickly ran to his father, who was lying on the ground bleeding from the neck area and barely able to speak. Gain yelled, "Help! Help!" Some who heard the commotion had already called 911, and were attending to Allen. He was dying, and knew there was not much time, so, he looked directly at his son, held his hand, and said, "Sometimes life allows you to see others as more important than yourself. When that happens, you will do all you can to help. I love you, son." At that moment, Gain saw his father close his eyes for the very last time. Alicia, Allen's wife, was taking a shower at the time of the attack, and had no clue of what had happened until it was too late ... to even say goodbye.

In the 6 years Allen and Alicia were married, many great times were shared in their household; both together and with Gain. To say that Allen's death was tough for Alicia is a serious understatement. It wasn't because she would miss building more enjoyable memories with him. There was just so much more she wanted to learn about him. She knew he loved her, but he lived his life as though he didn't need her. "How fitting was it," Alicia thought, "that Allen's death would be so sudden and bring about more mystery ... Where did the dog come from ... why Allen ... why now ... why did I not get a chance to say goodbye?"

The Little Helper

Almost three years had passed, but Gain's mother, Alicia, was still deeply saddened by the death of her husband. On several occasions, some of her friends advised her to get out of the house more and try to do a bit more than work, take care of Gain, and sleep. Alicia hardly ate and very seldom did she socialize with anyone other than those who were very close to her. She loved Allen so much that she just couldn't think of loving someone else in the same way. Gain, on the other hand, very talkative and playful. He loved his father just as much as his mom did, but because he was so young when his father died, he was able to "bounce back" after a few months. For those times he did get sad, he would right away do what his mom told him: think about the good times he spent with his father. Boy, were there a lot of good times. Gain was an only child, so his time with his parents was not split up between siblings. More than that, his parents believed in spending a great deal of quality time with their son. Therefore, it did not take long for Gain to think of something good he did with his father, and before long, he wasn't sad anymore.

Allen's mom was another source of joy in Gain's life, before and after the death of her son, but especially after. She decided that it would be better for her to do something than to sit home and think about Allen being gone, so she volunteered to help out at a homeless shelter almost every Saturday, and on most of those occasions she took Gain along with her. He even learned how to help out. Little did his grandmother, his mother, or anyone else know that those experiences at the shelter, coupled with Allen's last words spoken to him, that he should help others, at least that's how Gain understood it, would help to shape Gain's view about life in an absolutely amazing way.

Not more than six months after Allen's death, Alicia began to notice Gain wanting to do little chores around the house. Then he wanted to help the lawn man, and before long, he was the Best Teachers' Helper. Alicia didn't know if that was a real title or if Gain just made it up, so she asked Gain's teacher during a conference. Sure enough, the school, not only his teacher, gave Gain this title because he was consistently, genuinely helpful. Being so helpful at such a young age was, in itself, quite weird, but even stranger was the fact that in all of his helpfulness, Gain was never taken advantage of. He never went home from school or aftercare, telling his mom that he was hungry because he had given all of his food away to kids who said they had nothing to eat. He never needed an abundance of school supplies to give to the other students, and his mother never saw him exhausted from being overworked.

Gain was good at being helpful, not just because he liked to help others, but also because he knew whom to help.

ESCAPING DEATH

There were many occasions where kids would try to misuse Gain's generosity, but they were never ever successful. Not only would they try to get something from Gain by acting "needy," but some of the older kids would try to trick him. There was one instance where a boy wanted to scare Gain out of his wits. His name was Tommy. He was in the fifth grade and was jealous of Gain. He did not like the idea of a second grader getting more attention than him. So Tommy and a few of his friends decided that they would trap Gain inside a boarded-up doghouse that had a hole in it, through which Gain could fit, but not Tommy or his friends. The doghouse was located right next to the aftercare building.

Now Gain had never been tricked before. It was almost as if he could literally read people's minds. So this time would be no different. For Tommy and the gang, the day had finally come. They were going to put this little helper dude in his place. Over the weekend, when no one was there, Tommy had brought a board from home that was large enough to seal the hole after Gain crawled in. He had it resting on the side of the doghouse. About ten minutes after the children were allowed to go outside, Tommy ran over to Gain and, as if in desperation, told Gain that he and his friends needed his help. He said, "Me and my friends were playing catch with my big brother's baseball, and Pete— pointing at his friend— accidentally threw it into the boarded-up doghouse. We need you to crawl into the hole in the side to get my brother's ball. You're small enough to fit through the hole." Eventhough Gain was one of the tallest kids in his class; he was still relatively small in comparison Tommy and his friends. So, Gain looked at Tommy, smiled, and said, "Okay, I'll help."

When they got over to the doghouse, Gain started to get a strong feeling that something bad was about to happen. So he asked, "Tommy, can you look inside of the hole to make sure that nothing is in there?" Then Tommy, wanting to be extra convincing, said to Gain, "Yeah, sure, I'll even stick my head in the hole so you can see that it's not scary." As Tommy stuck his head into the hole, he noticed something shiny and thought in his mind that it may be a half-dollar coin. So he forgot all about the plan and focused only on the getting that coin. He took his right hand and arm and squeezed it through the hole while his head was still inside. He had no idea that he would get lodged inside, but that was exactly what happened. Tommy grabbed the coin and was about to pull his head out when he noticed that his head and arm could not move. He also noticed that when he attempted to crawl back, something would poke him either in the head or the arm. There were a few nails that had been hammered into the side of the doghouse which were sticking out and giving Tommy a very hard time. Tommy was stuck. Before long, this big fourth grader was screaming, "Help! I can't get out! I'm stuck! Can somebody help me?" One of the aftercare workers heard the noise and ran quickly over to where the kids were and, after about ten minutes, finally got Tommy out of the hole.

Gain's helpfulness was a strength, which sort of protected him and guided him through life. Gain, however, didn't think much of it. He just figured that was how he was supposed to live. His mom asked him once, "Gain, honey, do you ever get tired of helping people? I mean, you are so young, don't you think that you should be playing a lot more?" "I do play a lot, Mommy," Gain said happily. "I have lots of friends that I play with, and I play with you sometimes, I play with Uncle Phil and I play with—" "Okay, honey," Gain's mother said, interrupting his list of play friends. "Mommy," Gain said in a gentle voice, "do you like it when I help you?" His mom perked up and said, "Oh, yes! I love it when you help me. I am always amazed at how much work we get done together in such a little amount of time. So yes, darling, yes, I really enjoy your help!" Gain leaned over and gave his mom a hug and said, "Well, I think other people like my help too." Alicia smiled, rubbed his head, looked directly into his eyes, and said, "You're right, honey, you are absolutely right."

One month later, on a night when Gain's mom thought that he was asleep, Gain walked into the living room and saw her holding a picture of his dad in her hand while she cried softly. He didn't disturb her, because he knew why she was crying. This was by no means the first time he saw his mom in this way, but for some reason this time, Gain felt moved to do something about it. Perhaps, it was starting to make him feel sad. So in order for his mom to feel happy again, Gain felt he needed to help. He determined in his mind that he was going to find his mom a new husband.

Gain's project started with his uncle Phil. No, he did not ask his uncle to marry his brother's wife (although it would not have been illegal). He went to his uncle to ask him questions about how people get married, how they fall in love, and who might be a good "new husband" for his mother. Needless to say, his uncle was stunned that his seven-year-old nephew would ask such questions. Nevertheless, he answered Gain's questions and offered him some excellent advice. He said, "Gain, when the time comes that your mom starts thinking about marrying someone else, make sure that he loves your mother and you more than his job, his money, or any of his hobbies. You got that?" "Yes, sir!" said the happy-spirited Gain Watson to his uncle Phil, who knew that Gain was a unique kid but decided to keep a close watch on him just to make sure that everything was okay.

Two days after his talk with his uncle, Gain had a talk with the lawn man. A day later, he had a talk with one of his mom's co-workers who would stop in every now and then to see if Alicia needed any help around the house. A couple days later, Gain had a talk with his PE teacher, Coach Lampley. All three of these men were single, thirty-something, and had been very much involved in Gain's life, and every once in a while, they each shared a laugh or two with Alicia, who was twenty-nine.

Well, as stated earlier, Gain possessed some sort of ability to read the minds of the people he encountered. This gift proved to be very helpful when Gain talked to the three bachelors. Before you could turn your head, he had figured out who it was that his mother should marry: Coach Lampley, whose first name was Steve. He had always been fond of Alicia ever since he found out that she was raising Gain all by herself and doing a good job at it. All Gain had to do was find a way for his mother to agree to go out with Steve.

One evening, about a week after Steve had been selected as the suitor, Gain and his mom were watching a movie together, when out of the blue (so it seemed to Gain's mother), Gain asked, "Mom, do you think it will ever be okay for you to have another husband?" Alicia looked surprised that her son would ask such a question, but she was not at all upset.

After gathering her composure and clearing her throat, she said in the voice of an old Asian guru, "Oh, wise one, you do ask a tough question." They both laughed, and Alicia continued, "You know what, honey, it's funny you ask me that question now, because had you asked me a month ago, I would have definitely said no. But two weeks ago, I sat in this chair, holding a picture of your father, as I cried myself to sleep. Do you know why I was crying?" "Because you were sad and wanted Daddy to come back?" answered Gain. "Well, yes and no. Yes, I was sad, but it was not because I wanted Daddy to come back. I do miss him, and I always will, but the reason I was crying was because for the very first time, I chose to let him go." "But he was already gone, Mommy," Gain said. Alicia chuckled, saying, "No, sweetie, when I say 'let him go,' I mean that I'm going to stop thinking that he should be here with me." "Oohh, I get it now," Gain replied. "Gain, I love your father, and I always will, he'll at all times have a special place in my heart, but to answer your question, yes, I do think it will be okay for me to have another husband. I'm just a little nervous about going out and trying to meet someone and live a normal life." Gain smiled at his mom, and she smiled back. Then Gain said, "You'll be fine, Mommy." Alicia put her arm around her son and pulled him in close to her body, and as they continued watching the movie, the two of them fell asleep together on the couch.

As the weekend passed, Gain was excited about talking to Coach Lampley, so on Monday morning, before school started, Gain found Coach Lampley and asked him if he could come by the house on Thursday, just to "hang out" with him and his mom. Being that he had always wanted to spend more time with Gain and Alicia, Coach Lampley said in a mellow tone, trying to contain his abundance of excitement, "Sure, Gain. That seems like a lot of fun. What time shall I come over?" "Ummm, let's see," said Gain with a little bit of nervousness and anticipation in his voice. "I know we always get home from aftercare at five o'clock. How about—" He paused for a moment and then said with confidence, raising his index finger in the air as if he had come up with a bright idea, "Five-O-five!" Coach Lampley laughed a little, "Wow! Aren't we eager and anxious?" the coach said. "I tell you what," he continued. "Why don't we give you and your mom a little time to relax before I come over? How about 5:45 p.m.?" Gain, still excited, said "Okay, Coach!" as he walked away and went to his classroom.

That Thursday evening would turn out to be the best time that Alicia and Gain had since Allen died. Sense it was a school night, and it was just the three of them, Steve brought over a variety of Chinese food and a couple of board games that he figured they would all be able to play. As Gain had already told his mom that Coach Lampley was coming over, Alicia was prepared when she heard the door bell ring. This time, she was a little nervous instead of annoyed at the though of Steve coming over, and whe she opened the door, seeing the food in his hands, her nervousness changed to relief. She really did not want to have to cook. She greeted Steve with a warm smile, and allowed him to come in.

"Thanks for bringing us dinner, Steve," said Alicia. "You know you really did not have to." Steve responded, "I know, I just figured this would give us more time to have fun ... right Gain?" as he smiled and lifted up the board games. "That's right, coach!" answered Gain. And after a few hours of food, fun and even charades, Alicia sent Gain to prepare for bed. As he went on his way, he told the two of them goodnight. They responded "goodnight."

When Gain left, Steve, wanting so badly to stay, did not want to give the impression that he only hung out with Gain for the sake of winning Alicia's heart and spending more time with her, so he stood up and said, "Well, sense all the fun is gone now, I guess I'll leave too. Alicia's mouth dropped. Even though she was not in a rush to get into a relationship, and at times was not the most pleasant person to be around; mourning the loss of her husband, this time she actually tried, and, well … genuinely enjoyed herself. Immediately, Steve noticed that she was not too pleased with his comment, so he plainly told her, "I'm sorry. That was a bad joke, but I was just kidding. While Gain is very likeable, amusing, and a really great kid, you were my main focus this evening, and honestly, the real reason it was so exciting." Alicia was moved by his words, but still curious, so she asked, "So why did you say it? Why did those sweet words you just said not come out first?" "It was my way of suppressing my own feelings, that right now, may not be helpful to our relationship," said Steve. Smiling, Alicia responded, "I understand. You don't want to rush things … and I thank you for that, because I do have mixed feelings about this, but I know it's good for me as well as Gain." With that being said, she walked Steve to the door, gave him a quick, but thoughtful hug, and they said goodnight to each other.

Little by little, as Steve and Alicia continued to get to know each other better, Alicia's comfort level began to rise, and her mixed feelings began to subside. Her problem, which

Steve was very sensitive to, was that she did not want to forget about Allen. She felt guilty about enjoying another man's company the way she did with her husband, but after a while, they were spending every weekend together. Soon after that, Steve would periodically go grocery shopping with Gain and Alicia. Then Steve and Alicia would go out on dates by themselves. They enjoyed each other so much, and it was obvious that Alicia had fallen in love with Steve, and Steve had fallen in love with Alicia and Gain.

By now, two more years had passed, and Steve, Alicia, and Gain knew that the time was right for them to be known as the Lampleys. Steve proposed to Alicia three days after his birthday. Alicia accepted his proposal for marriage, and four months later, they were wedded. Three years after they were married, one month after their anniversary, they had a baby together, a girl, whom they named Angela. Though Alicia and Steve had there normal, typical struggles in marriage, one thing Alicia noticed was that they communicated so much better than her and Allen did. Before they were even married, Steve had revealed more about himself, his dreams, his fears, his challenges at work, and much more than Allen had allowed Alicia to know in the whole time they were together. Alicia and Gain were finally experiencing the "good life" they had lost when Allen died.

It's Time for a Change

One day, when Gain, almost thirteen now, was walking home from the park, his mom saw him do something that shocked her so much so that she had a physical reaction and frightening experience to what she saw. As Gain walked along the sidewalk, he noticed a little girl playing with her puppy in the yard. Well, what the little girl didn't know was that her little furry friend was going to run out into the street and that there was a large pickup truck coming down the street to smash it. Gain, however, was watchful of the little girl and her puppy. Within seconds, the puppy dashed out of the yard and into the street. The driver of the truck could not see him, so he didn't stop nor slow down. The puppy saw the truck coming and froze, and at that very moment, while the little girl gasped and covered her face with her hands, Gain ran into the street, picked up the puppy, and jumped onto the grass beside the street. Gain was so close to getting hit by the truck that the front tire nearly grazed the bottom of his shoe as he dove out of the way. The little girl was so happy and scared at the same time that she gave Gain a big hug, took her puppy, and ran into her house, saying "Thank you!" as she ran.

Alicia saw the whole thing, and for the very first time in all the years of Gain's life, she realized that he was not invincible. She began to think about what would have happened if the truck had hit her son. This thought caused her to get a little bit woozy, and within five seconds, Alicia fainted and fell onto the front lawn. Gain didn't see his mother faint, but as he got a little closer to the house, he saw her lying on the grass. Immediately, Gain had a flashback of his father lying on the ground in the backyard. He started running, crying, and yelling all at the same time. "Mom!" he yelled, and upon reaching her, he yelled, "Somebody help!" Steve came running out of the house. Looking her over, he noticed that she was breathing but was a little pale. He concluded that she had fainted and told Gain to go get a small pot of cold water and to put a rag inside it. Then after Gain had returned, he told him to go inside and keep an eye on Angela. She was in her playpen. Steve applied the damp rag to Alicia's forehead, and her eyes began to open as she muttered softly, "What just happened?" Then as she saw that Steve was kneeling over her, she became a little frantic, asking, "Steve, did I faint?" Continuing to hold her hand and reassure her that everything was okay, as he waved off neighbors who had come by to help, Steve said, "Alicia, you're doing just fine. I'm going to let you lie here for a few more minutes, then I'll help you into the house, and yes, you did faint." As she lay there, Alicia told Steve what happened. She said, "Gain was almost hit by a big truck, as he saved a puppy from being smashed. It frightened me. I was overwhelmed, Steve. If our son is going to continue to do things like this, there is no guarantee that he'll never fall short and meet the same fate as his father. We've got to do something, I'm not ready to lose him."

That night, Steve had a talk with Gain. The two of them were sitting in Gain's room after they had eaten dinner. Gain asked, "Is Mom feeling better?" "Oh, yeah, she's doing fine," Steve replied. Gain smiled and said, "Good, now I feel better." Steve closed his eyes for a moment and bent his head down as if in deep thought. Gain was a little worried about Steve, so he asked, "Dad"—Gain had decided early on to call Steve "Dad" even before he was adopted—"are you okay?" Steve lifted his head, smiled a little, and said, "Son, I want you to know that I love you, and everything I do for you, with you, or even to you is because I love you." Gain was getting a little nervous hearing his father talk like this, so he jumped in before he could finish. "Okay, Dad, is something weird about to happen? You're not going to leave us, are you?" Steve placed his hand on Gain's shoulder, looked him in the eyes, smiled, and said, "That would be extremely painful for me. You know I can't live without you guys." No longer smiling, Steve continued, "I am, however, going to say something that you may not like, but you're going to have to trust me." "Okay, I'm ready," said Gain.

Steve went on to say, "Your mom saw you today walking home from the park. She saw what you did for the little girl." He paused and took a breath in and out. "Gain, the reason your mother was lying on the ground is because she fainted at the thought of losing someone else she loved. While it was a very nice thing to do, it gave your mother one of the worst feelings she had ever felt. She thought that truck was going to run over you, and there was nothing that she could have done to help you." Then Gain, attempting to set his father's mind at rest, said with a bit of inflection in his voice, "Dad, I was fine. I wasn't really worried about the truck. I just wanted to save the puppy." "And that's the problem, son!" Steve said in a moderately loud voice. Realizing his loudness, he paused for a second or two and continued in a calm but intense voice, "You were only thinking about the puppy and the little girl. You forgot to think about yourself. What if you would have gotten hit by the truck? At best, you would have been in the hospital for a few days, but you could very likely have been killed."

Gain thought about how long it took for his mother to get past his father's death. He was silent, but his mind continued to talk to him. He thought about his father's dying words: do all you can to help others. Then he thought about what his life would be like if he had never heard those words from his father. "Gain, were you listening to me?" Steve asked. Gain was so deep in thought that it wasn't until Steve called him three times that he responded. "Oh, I'm sorry, Dad. What you said about Mom just caught me off guard." The two were silent for a few seconds. Then Gain asked, "So what is it that you want me to do, Dad?"

Steve got up and began to pace the floor, thinking about how to say what was in his heart. Then, still standing, Steve turned toward Gain and said, "Gain, I've always thought of your unusual desire to help others as a gift or something. I've never met a child like you, and I'm sure not many people have. Now that you're getting older, bigger, and stronger, I'm afraid that the situations you encounter will get increasingly dangerous. I no longer view your helpfulness as a gift, but as a curse." Immediately, Gain's head dropped. Noticing Gain's countenance, Steve kneeled down and lifted Gain's head by his chin and continued. He said, "Son, I am not saying that your father cursed you, nor am I saying that you were not supposed to do the things you did. I'm just saying that maybe now that you have a father again, you can go on and live a regular life. Perhaps, all your dad was trying to tell you was to be there for your mom and grow up to be a responsible man." Gain started to perk up a bit and sat up, as if a weight had been lifted off his shoulders. Steve, preparing to end the conversation, said, "Gain, I'm here now. I'm responsible for this family, which includes you. From this day forward—"

Suddenly, they heard Alicia yell out, "Steve! There's someone at the door!" This was strange, because it was nearly eight o' clock and they weren't expecting anyone. "Who could that be?" Steve mumbled, and as he left Gain's room, he said, "Gain, we'll finish this up later, okay?" "Sure, Dad," said Gain.

As Steve got to the door, he looked through the peephole and saw that there was a gentleman, appearing to be in his mid fifties, clean shaven, with mixed grey and black hair, standing about 6 feet tall, and medium build, outside. Sensing no threat of danger, Steve opened the door. "May I help you?" Steve said. "Yes, if you are the parent of a young man named Gain Lampley, you can help me," the man responded. Feeling a little apprehensive about giving out any personal information, but at the same time curious about how this man knew his son, Steve said, "I'm Gain's father. Is everything all right with him?" With a little more excitement in his voice, the man responded, "Oh yes, yes, everything is going extremely well with Gain. One could consider this as a 'good news' visit, and if you'd allow me to come in, I'll tell you exactly why I'm here." By now, Alicia was standing behind Steve, so he turned to her to make sure that she would be fine with the man coming in for a moment. Being curious herself, Alicia said, "I'll be fine."

As the man came in, he introduced himself as Edward Wilde. Steve and Alicia introduced themselves also. After they had sat down, Mr. Wilde began his explanation of the visit. "First of all, I am sorry for perhaps startling you with my late, unplanned visit. It's just that time is of essence." Alicia and Steve gave each other concerned looks as Mr. Wilde continued, "I am one of the first graduates of LIFE Academy, LIFE being an acronym for League of Intellectuals Fostering Excellence. It has been in existence for over thirty years, yet not too many people know of us or what we're all about. Now I'm going to tell you a little bit about what we do. Sounds good?" "Sure, we have some time," said Steve. Alicia agreed as well.

Mr. Wilde began, "LIFE Academy was formed by a professor who had become tired of teaching students to a 'standard.' He believed that the government served to restrain, and since most schools were regulated by the government, he insisted that students were not able to do what they were born to do. He wanted to help students reach their full potential in life with no limitations, and since its conception, the league has done nothing short of bringing out the absolute best in all of its students, all of whom, with no exceptions, excel to the top of their professions. LIFE graduates stand alone."

"This is all good information, I guess. But what does this have to do with Gain, our son?" Alicia asked. "Oh, I am terribly sorry, and I promise that I won't take up much more of your time," Edward said, pepping up a bit as he thought about the possibility of having Gain attend the academy. He continued, "I was told a a couple of years ago, by one of the members of the league, who had interacted regularly with Gain, that he was a possible candidate for attending LIFE Academy. You know this informant as Phil, Gains uncle. Steve and Alicia's eyes opened as wide as quarters, and both said in unison, "Phil!" "I'm sorry. I should have told you from the beginning, Alicia, that your brother-in-law is not only a graduate of LIFE Academy, but he's also an active member of the Life League, through which all of our support comes. The Life League insures that the academy lacks nothing, whether, money, material resources, teachers, trainers, or even enrollment. As I said, LIFE graduates excel to the tops of their professions. Supporting the academy is no strain at all for Life League members, in fact, it's an honor. We'll talk more on that later."

Mr. Wilde continued, "Having received Phil's recommendation, we began to watch him carefully and what we've noticed over the past year or so, is that your son is an extremely busy boy. What you saw earlier today is just a normal part of his life." Puzzled, Steve asked, "Earlier today … what happened earlier today?" Mr. Wilde responded, "I assure you that all we do is monitor behaviors, and we do have legal clearance to do so for the sake of determining who might be a good fit for the Academy." Getting a little nervous, anxious, and worried Alicia said, "We understand that, but what happened earlier today? Was it the truck incident?"

"Don't be alarmed, because fact is, your son is very unique, and in all my years of being here at the Academy. Just to let you know, your son has not only saved the lives of animals, but peoples lives as well; pulling them out of harm's and alerting them of unforeseen danger. You're not gonna want to hear this, but there was a time when three older guys tried to physically bully him as he walked home from school, and they couldn't lay a hand on him. It wasn't because he ran, but because he maneuvered his way around them as if he had eyes behind his back. Finally they tired of trying to get him, and went home. He possesses some sort of extra sense that alerts him of impending harm, and an ability to react to it appropriately. This is what he was made to do. *Remove this green section* Steve jumped in, "From our stand point, Mr. Wilde, you came to our home uninvited and began to tell us that you are a part of a special club with a practically unknown location, whose members spy on innocent children."

Alicia asked, "So you're saying that Phil wants to enroll Gain into this academy?" "No, Mr. and Mrs. Lampley," Mr. Wilde said. "It's the academy that wants to enroll your son. He is the gifted intellectual for whom this academy was founded. Leaving his educational life in the hands of mainstream schooling would be nothing short of catastrophic. Your son, Gain, must have more." Besides eventually, if his skills are not harnessed and given a direct purpose, one day he may end up falling short or moving out of the way a little too late. Or who knows, maybe these guys will never stop trying to get him and one day succeeds.

Steve looked at Alicia (both of them shrugging their shoulders so as to say it's something that they might consider), and said, "So Allen knew nothing of this?" Alicia responded, "If he did, he would never have told me. This is the type of stuff that he would not envolve me in. I'm surprised though, I never would have thought of Phil as being in something like this. We're definitely going to have a tald." Turning back to Mr. Wilde, Steve said, "Well, this is a lot to swallow in such a short period of time. Your offer is tempting because we only want the best for our son, and we want to keep him safe, but Alicia and I have to talk it over with one another and then with Gain. Do you have anything we can look at or read to learn more about LIFE Academy?"

As they all stood up and began walking to the door, Mr. Wilde reached into his inside coat pocket, taking out a brochure and handing it to Steve, saying, "Guard this carefully. The league considers it as an exclusive, members-only peek into the academy. No one else can see it except the three of you. We prefer to do our own recruiting. I'll be back in a week to get it as well as your answer." Cautiously holding on to the brochure, Steve opened the door for Mr. Wilde as they bid each other good night. When the door closed, Alicia ran over to call Phil, who confirmed that everything was as Mr. Wilde had said. However, he did not tell her much more about the academy nor the Life League.

While all of this was happening, Gain was in his room, pondering over the conversation he had with Steve. He was torn between opinions. On one hand, he was happy at the thought of becoming a normal kid with normal responsibilities, but on the other hand, deep down inside, he really couldn't imagine himself changing. In part, Gain did not want to change, and Gain, just like any other kid, began to dream of being a superhero. Also, the manner in Allen died (saving his son's life and sacrificing his) allowed Gain, as he got older, to reason that his father was a hero as well. How then could he not honor his father's last words? This was Gain's dilemma. Thinking so hard made him get a little tired, so he changed his clothes got into his bed and went to sleep.

The next morning, after Steve and Alicia had spent almost the entire night discussing whether or not they should allow Gain to attend the academy, they talked with Gain in the living room while little Angela continued to sleep. Both parents had agreed that Gain would make the final decision, because having him attend the academy had its pros and cons. The academics were extremely superior, and the activities such as martial arts and information technology were top-notch. However, students were only allowed to see their families one weekend a month and two weeks during the summer. Together, the three of them read through the brochure and determined that although attending the academy would mean that Gain would not be able to see much of his family, passing up such an opportunity was not something he was willing to do. Gain was absolutely thrilled at the idea. Though he was quite popular in elementary school, Gain had become a bit of a loner in middle school. The kids just did not want to hang around a person who did so much good. More than that, he thwarted many pranks some students had planned against both teachers and other students. He just didn't fit in. Therefore, they all determined that it would be best for Gain to attend and graduate from LIFE Academy. Alicia and Steve were saddened by the fact that he would be gone so much, but they were also relieved. "Well, honey," Alicia said to Steve as Gain left to go to his room, "at least we don't have to worry about him jumping out in front of any more trucks." Steve held her closely, and they both smiled.

What Mom Doesn't Know

"Selena, I'm on my way," Gain said through his hands-free communication device. "Crash!" As Gain hurled himself out of the first-floor window of an abandoned warehouse occupied by drug dealers, Selena, his partner, was waiting for him in the car. Quickly, Gain jumped into the car and the two of them sped away. A couple of the men who had chased after Gain fired shots at the vehicle but missed completely. "How did it go in there?" Selena asked as she drove back to the League Elite headquarters. Gain looked at her, slowly smiling, and said, "The Flea has been launched." "Yes!" Selena replied.

The Flea, technically named the HDSRC 15003, which stood for Homing Device Superior Remote Controlled, was the most advanced and complex tracking device in the world. Designed and created by LIFE Academy graduates, Lance Wilson and Greg Horn, the Flea got its name because it was a little bit smaller than a flea and, by remote control, moved along a person's body at will, undetected by any of the senses. Once discharged and attached to the host, the Flea, which was controlled by Ryan Cummings, another graduate of

LIFE Academy, would make its way to the host's fingertips to scan for identity. After scanning, it would begin to video and voice record all events encountered by the host. As a homing device, the Flea was detectable up to four hundred miles underground and could be detected at any distance through any wall above ground.

Gain's job was to deploy the Flea, causing an attachment to a man suspected as being Floyd Grimeson, a.k.a. the "Sting," who was the number 1 distributor of drugs on the entire West Coast of the United States. Through the Intelligence Division of League Elite, Gain and Selena were able to locate the Sting's whereabouts (the abandoned warehouse). This was not a drug bust; Gain's purpose was to get close enough to the Sting so that he could take a picture of him. He could be no more than fifteen feet away, because the camera flash, which was used to set the Flea in motion, though it could discharge and attach to its host at the speed of light, would disintegrate after a very short distance if not engaged with the host.

Facing a warehouse full of drug dealers was nothing for Gain as long as he had an escape route, and when it came to escaping, none did it better than Gain. As he hid behind a few large wooden crates, he noticed a window, which was about twenty yards away. Communicating to Selena the location of the window, he told her to have the car ready. "On it," Selena replied. Gain took one more peek around the crate to make sure that he would have the proper angle to take the picture. "Good," he whispered to himself. Making no noise at all, he put on his goggles. Then he got into position and jumped out into the opening, where he snapped a perfect picture of the

Sting. While still in the air, Gain heard Ryan say in his earpiece, "The Flea has attached," and he spun three times before hitting the ground. As he spun, smoke bombs that were loosely attached to his clothing dislodged and began to explode on impact. This created a roomful of smoke, and no one could see except for Gain because of his goggles. Then he ran, jumped through the window, and he and Selena got away.

Back at the headquarters, all of the League Elite members were excited about the fact that the Flea was working as planned. The fingerprint scan had confirmed the man as Floyd Grimeson. Also, they were already receiving important information from the conversations held by the Mr. Grimeson. Now the League Elite team consisted of ten members, all graduates of LIFE Academy, each of whom went on to graduate number one or number two in class from the top universities and colleges in the world. However, it was not their excellence in academics alone that qualified these young men and women to be a part of the League Elite team. Students of LIFE Academy were taught in five areas: academics (of course), martial Arts (all forms), information technology, advanced gadgetry, and survival skills. In order to be considered a League Elite eligible, these young learners had to rank in the top three of each of the five areas at the time of graduation. Once the top three were selected, there was one more factor for determination that had to be unanimously obvious to all of the LIFE League board members. The final element that a potential League Elite member had to possess was a unique skill or gift: Lance Wilson and Greg Horn, inventors; Ryan Cummings, decoder; Selena Tolson, mechanics; Gain Lampley, agility; Norris Nichols and Cameron Wheeler, tracking; Robert Govers and Amy Priscle, intelligence; Jacquelyn Frands, interpretation. This was the League Elite, which was directed by none other than Mr. Edward Wilde, whose mind was set on eliminating the sell and use of illegal drugs worldwide. He finally had a team that he felt could actually get it done.

"Hello," Gain said as he picked up his phone. "Hi, stranger, how are you doing?," a voice said. "Mom," Gain responded. "Yes, it's me," his mom said and continued, "I just felt like hearing my son's voice, since he had deserted his family and gone on to bigger and better things: new dreams, new job, new home, new state…" "Well, aren't you the funny one?" Gain said cheerfully. "So when is the next time we can expect to see you?" his mom asked. Gain responded, "Well, I was going to try and surprise you guys by just showing up, but since you've asked, how about tomorrow evening?" "Tomorrow evening!" his mom replied with excitement. Continuing on, she said, "Tomorrow evening would be wonderful! We'll have a big dinner waiting for you. Oh, and see if you can bring Selena with you." "I'll see what I can do, Mom," Gain said, smiling inside. "I love you, son," she said. "I love you too, Mom," he answered.

Now it just so happened that Mr. Wilde, desiring to reward the team for a job well done and to allow time for relaxation and preparation for the next mission, granted the League Elite members a full week off from having to work. Therefore, not wanting to squander his time hanging around his house, Gain decided to fly home even before his mom had called, but because she called and made a special request, he'd take Selena as well, who too wanted to get out of Washington for a while.

All the league members had very flexible undercover jobs appointed to them by the Life League. Gain was a high-level IT consultant for one of Life League's software firms. Selena was one of their accountants. Neither of Gain's parents knew anything about the League Elite. Both Gain and Selena felt that if his parents did know about it, they would definitely not approve of it. Gain and Selena had been friends ever since they enrolled in the academy. They enjoyed each other's company so much that during the last two summers at the academy, they spent their two weeks together at Gain's house.

Selena did not know of her parents. She was abandoned by her mother at the age of three and had been in various foster-care homes up until she was selected to attend the academy. Selena was an exceptional child who had a fascination with figuring out how machines work. It did not matter what the machine was; from toys to sewing machines to cars, she wanted to get her hands on it and see what made it tick. This enthrallment with gadgets, however, was a double-edged sword, because even though she learned a lot from taking things apart and putting them back together, her foster parents' valuables were being destroyed in the process.

Eventually, time after time, she would be taken back to the orphanage. Still, she continued to do the same thing with every house. Her counselors thought of her actions as sort of a defense mechanism to protect her from being let down again. However, when she turned ten, she had figured out how to completely disassemble and reassemble a car engine. The foster parents who took her at that time had an older son, a mechanic who always worked on cars in their backyard. He taught Selena so much, and she began to like it there.

The problem came when she became so good that the family started putting her to work and making money off this "young Einstein" of a girl. This went on for about a year and a half before the orphanage found out about it. Consequently, they removed her from the only home she kind of enjoyed.

About that same time, the LIFE League was canvassing the area for potential students. When they stopped by the orphanage and heard about Selena, it took no time at all for her to be transferred over to the custody of the academy. LIFE Academy was by its very nature a foster-care facility, which was well equipped to handle all of Selena's needs. The very moment she sat foot on the campus, Selena realized that the academy was where she was supposed to be. She loved it and benefited from everything they had to offer. When she started visiting Gain's house, she felt a love in that home that she had never felt before. They became like parents to her, though she always saw Gain as a friend, her best friend. Steve and Alicia kept a close eye on them while they visited, making sure that nothing beyond friendship would go on, even though at the time, neither one of them had any sort of romantic feelings for the other. Notwithstanding, anyone (except Selena and Gain) could clearly see that they were well made for each other. Presently, Gain is two weeks into his twenty-fourth year of life, and Selena is twenty-three years, eleven months, and fifteen days young.

Seeds of Love

"Gain, you really should let me drive. I know I can get us to the airport on time, but as for you—" Interrupting Selena, Gain said, "As for me I can get us there on time, and I'll do it without sparking any attention from the 'blue light crew.'" Selena gasped, because she could not believe that Gain would actually remind her of the only time she had ever gotten a ticket, and she didn't really think that she was speeding. Then she said in a mildly upset voice, "Well, I sure hope you're right, mister. 'I love driving like a turtle.'" Gain, attempting to make light of the situation, responded in a calm almost comforting voice, "Selena, I'm sorry, but turtles don't drive." While trying to hold back a laugh, Selena said, "Gain, you have absolutely no sense at all."

As it turns out, the two did arrive on time to the airport and made it to Gain's parents' house a couple hours before dinner. As the doorbell rang, Angela, who was the most excited, yelled out, "I'll get it!" After she opened the door, her eyes opened wide, and she gave Selena a big hug. Then she took her by the hand and said, "Come on! I want to show you something in my room." As they were headed for the room, Angela, remembering her brother was home too, shouted, "Hi, Gain, love you!" At about the same time, Gain's parents were coming out of the family room, so when Selena saw them, she (still being pulled by Angela) quickly said, "Hi, Mr. and Mrs. Lampley! We'll hug later!" The two laughed as Alicia said, "Okay, Selena! Anyway, it's good to see you!"

By now, Gain had brought both his and Selena's bags into the living room, and as he sat the bags down, he walked over to his parents and gave them hugs, saying, "Mom, Dad, it's so good to see you. It's been about eight months since we last saw each other. What have I missed?" Steve said, "Well, son, you haven't missed much, although we did have another Christmas vacation. We left about three weeks after you returned home from our Thanksgiving dinner." Gain's eyes lit up as he said, "Oh, I remember the Christmas vacation. Wow, that had to have been at least ten years ago." "Thirteen years ago, you were eleven," Alicia said. "And since Angie is eleven now, we figured we'd do it again." Then, as though bubbling with anticipation, Steve interjected, "Okay, that's enough about us. What is going on with you?" Gain was a little nervous at the question, because just a couple days earlier, he was jumping out of a window, being chased by drug dealers with guns. Nevertheless, he gathered his thoughts and said, "I can honestly say that life if busy for me, but I love each and every moment of it. There is something, however, that I would like for you guys to keep a secret about Selena and me—" Beating Gain to the end of his statement, Steve, who had been waiting so long to see if the two would ever become more than just friends, said, "Is the secret that you have somehow become attracted to her, and you're wondering if you should maybe start dating her?"

"Yeah!" said Gain, as if surprised that his father knew exactly what he was going to say. Then he calmed down and continued, "I mean, you're right, Dad, she is becoming rather attractive to me and ... but our lives are so complicated."

As the three were talking, Selena, with Angela by her side, walked into the living room and officially greeted Gain's parents. After a round of hugs, smiles, and a bit of small talk, Gain and his father went to put the bags away. Selena would stay in the guestroom upstairs (Gain's old room), and Gain would stay in the guestroom downstairs. While the men were taking care of the luggage, Alicia turned to her daughter and said, "Angie, is it okay if I take Selena away from you for a little while? She and I have to 'catch up' on some things." "Sure, Mom," Angela replied, "I'll just go and watch a movie or something." "Thanks, sweetie," Alicia said. While she was walking toward the family room, Angela said, "Oh, and, Mom, I am almost old enough to know when the subject of boys or men is coming up, for now though, I'll pretend that I don't know you will be talking about Gain. But you know, I think they do make a good couple." Embarrassed a bit by Angela's comments, Selena said jokingly, "Mrs. Lampley, please tell me I'm not wearing a sign on my back that says, 'Gain is my sweetheart,' or 'I love you, Gain!' isn't written on my forehead, is it?" They both laughed and walked out onto the patio.

Meanwhile, Gain and his father were having a little discussion upstairs. "So what exactly did you mean when you said that your lives are complicated?" Steve asked. "Well, to be honest," Gain responded, "I'm not quite sure of what I meant, because there are days when we can talk about anything, laugh, and enjoy one another's company, and everything seems right.

But those are the times when I'm only thinking of her as my best friend. Lately though, I've been noticing how she laughs, how she smiles, how beautiful she is inside and out, and after a while, I don't talk normal. Then Selena doesn't know how to respond to me, and we end up getting mad at each other over absolutely nothing." Steve chuckled for a second or two and said, "Gain, your mother and I have been married for a little over fourteen years now, and there are still some times when we get mad at each other over absolutely nothing. But I'll tell you this. Every night, since I first fell in love with her, I've gone to sleep completely happy with the fact that she and I will be together until death separates us. Now what does that have to do with your situation with Selena?" Steve lowered his head as if thinking about an explanation. Then he lifted his head quickly and stared at Gain right in the eyes, putting his right hand on Gain's shoulder and saying with total confidence, "I don't know…" Then patting Gain on the back and with an upbeat tone in his voice, he said, "But let's go and shoot around a bit before dinner!" Gain laughed to himself, and they went outside to play basketball.

Around the same time the guys were talking, Alicia and Selena were talking. "Sooo, has my wonderful son shown any signs of being interested in more than just a friendship with you?" Selena responded with a hint of frustration and elevation in her voice, "Mrs. Lampley, I mean this with no disrespect to you or Mr. Lampley at all, but I really think Gain needs to stay home a bit and watch how you guys do this thing called love." Selena's statement caused Alicia to laugh, so she couldn't respond before Selena continued, who also wanted to laugh a little, but she held it back, saying, "I'm serious. I don't think he knows what he's doing." Alicia, still wanting to laugh, began to regain her composure, as Selena continued, "Okay, here is an example. Three weeks ago, Gain and I went to watch a movie together, and I was so excited and hopeful because it was his idea to go, and he actually called it a date. Well, as soon as he arrived to pick me up, I was ready and looking very attractive. I wasn't dressed up, but I'm not lying when I say I had it together. When I opened the door, and he saw me, do you know what your son said? He said, 'You know, I wouldn't want to marry you.'" Alicia's mouth dropped wide open. "Exactly, Mrs. Lampley, that's what he did," said Selena. "Here's the problem though. Gain told me that the reason he said it was because he was trying to say that I was so beautiful, that if he were married to me, it would be hard work trying to keep all the guys away." Relieved, Alicia's mouth closed, and laughing a little, she said, "You may be right, Selena, maybe he does need to stay home a bit." Selena laughed for a few seconds, then she took a deep breath in and out and said, "Mrs. Lampley, Gain does frustrate me sometimes, but I have honestly met no one who has been as good to me as he has. He is really an awesome friend, but as much as I want more than friendship, maybe that's all we'll ever be." "Hmm," said Alicia, "I've never really thought of you and Gain spending all this time together only to end up as friends, but it is very possible that you're right." *Those details come up later. I'm hoping I can get away with presenting it this way.*

Selena's countenance fell as Alicia continued, "I have to admit, I've been thinking of you as Gain's future wife ever since the first time you spent a part of your summer with us. Nevertheless, it isn't what I think that should determine your future, is it?" Selena responded in a soft, sad voice, "No, I guess not." Then after about ten seconds of silence, Alicia said, "Selena, just make sure that before you give in to just friendship, you can honestly say that you've put forth a worthy effort. Do not leave any issues unresolved or any questions unasked. You have to try." Selena started smiling, and after giving Alicia a hug, she said, "Okay, I won't give up yet, but can you do me just this one favor?" "Yes, anything," said Alicia. With a humorous voice of desperation, Selena said, "Pleeeaaassse, pray for Gain's communication skills!" They both laughed as they left the patio and returned to the living room.

That evening, they all sat and had a wonderful dinner together. It was just as always, lots of conversation, laughter, and fun. Angela even provided a little music on her flute. Though they genuinely enjoyed themselves, Selena and Gain were both a little troubled, so after things had settled down, Gain asked Selena if she would go for a walk with him, and she said yes. As it was customary when doing something with Selena that felt romantic, Gain started to get nervous. His first words after they began their walk were, "Boy, Selena, you sure did eat a lot in there," and in Selena's mind, she saw herself slap him *hard*. However, she remembered how Alicia told her that she must try and give a worthy effort. Therefore, rather than doing what was in her mind, or anything related, she responded by snorting two times like a pig and saying with a silly smile, "You didn't know Porky Pig was my great-great-grandfather, did ya?" And almost in disbelief, Gain started laughing. He was not only laughing because Selena was funny, but because he was so happy that his words did not start an argument. Immediately, Gain's began nervousness subsided, even though he still felt like he was on a date with Selena.

Something truly amazing happened to Gain. For the very first time in their lives together, the words, "I love you, Selena" were forming in his heart, waiting to be spoken. His laughter, which was more out of excitement than pure humor, continued, so Selena interrupted, "Hey, it's not that funny, is it?" Gain slowly stopped laughing until he was simply smiling at Selena. He said to her, "You really are as beautiful inside as you are on the outside." "Huh?" Selena was totally confused, but before she could say more, Gain continued, "I know…I know I just insulted you, and without missing a beat, I complimented you. I am perfectly aware of that fact, but let me tell you what just happened."

Selena was a little optimistic about Gain's next words, but just to be on the safe side, she prepared her mind for the worst. She had no clue as to what Gain was about to say, so she took in a deep breath, slowly exhaled, and said, "I'm ready." Walking Selena over to a bench, Gain said, "Just to let you know, I didn't even watch you eat, because my mind was somewhere else. But what I did notice a moment ago was how much you care for me." Selena smiled. Gain continued, "I said something that should have ruined a wonderful evening, but you chose not to let that happen. Obviously, you saw me as one drowning in nervousness and chose to cover my mistake. I do not know why that did it for me, but instantly, I felt free to express my true feelings about you." Taking Selena's hands and looking into her eyes, he said, "The second you gave in, I gave in and surrendered all of my fears about being more than just friends with you. I am no longer afraid of where this relationship will take us. I love you, Selena." With tears in her eyes, Selena said, "I love you too, Gain."

Making Adjustments

While Gain and Selena were on vacation, getting to know each other better, solid information about Floyd Grimeson, the Sting, was being gathered by the Flea. Angrily, Mr. Grimeson spoke, "No, I have no idea why someone would want to take a picture of me! We weren't doing anything illegal at the time, but I'm really starting to get steamed, because it feels like someone is trying to work me from the inside!" "So then, you know what you have to do, right?" said Jeff Spartan, who was the number 2 distributor of cocaine on the East Coast of the United States. *This is not the antagonist. These guys represent a portion of what the Life League does to help the country and establish trust from the government.* Mr. Grimeson responded, "I know what I should do. I should find out who it is and bury that person alive. I can't, though, because the biggest deal of the decade is in five days. I don't have time to test the loyalty of my men!" "What do you mean you don't have time?" said Mr. Spartan. "You do know that if you go ahead with the plan and ignore the problem, there is a huge chance that it won't be the biggest deal of the decade, but the biggest drug bust. Look,

Floyd, I understand how tempting it is to be careless, but we have to scrap the deal and come up with a different plan."

As Mr. Spartan regained his composure and Mr. Grimeson began to calm down, Mr. Spartan said, "Here, take this." Mr. Grimeson took a disc from Mr. Spartan's hand, asking, "What's this?" Mr. Spartan responded, "It's a lot of money, that's what it is." "What do you mean 'a lot of money'?" asked Mr. Grimeson. "I mean, the boss wants to give you and me an early Christmas present," said Mr. Spartan. Mr. Grimeson gave him a confused look. "It's like this," said Mr. Spartan. "There is some information on this disc that the boss wants delivered to some guy named Dennis. The address and directions are on the package. He gave this to me to give to you, and now he wants you to give it to Dennis." Mr. Spartan added, "When you get there, you're going to be checked for wires or hidden recorders. You will also have to give the secret password, 'locust and wild honey.' Once you've been cleared, this Dennis guy will come out and ask you for the disc. Do not say a word to him, only hand him the disc, and he will hand you two suitcases, each containing a large sum of money. Do not count the money! Take it directly to the dog-food warehouse, two miles south of Dennis's place. Two guys will meet you at precisely twelve o'clock noon. Do not be late! They will not search you, they will only ask you for the password. After you say it, hand the money over to them, and your job will be done. Do you have any questions?"

"I do have one question," said Mr. Grimeson. "Why is he sticking me with this job?" Spartan answered, "Because he knows you can get the job done." Angrily, Grimeson responded, "Yeah, but I'm too high up on the food chain to be doing flunky jobs like this!" "Too high up for a quarter of a million dollars?" asked Spartan. In disbelief, Grimeson said, "Stop playin', man! He is not giving up that kind of cheese for a little job like this!" Spartan answered, "Why not? He's getting three and a half million." "That makes me want to look at what's on the disc, but I won't," said Grimeson. "It's not that you won't look at the disc, you are forbidden," explained Spartan. Grimeson concluded, "The other job was bigger, but I don't know what kind of cut I was going to get. I'm good, now I'm ready for my two hundred and fifty thousand dollars."

Mr. Spartan ended the conversation with the final instructions. "Your first step is to book a flight to St. Louis. The arrival time has to be no later than nine o'clock in the morning, this coming Sunday. Dennis's home is approximately thirty miles east of the airport. Follow the directions carefully because you have to get there by ten thirty. If you suspect anything at all, break the disc in half and throw it away. Are you totally clear on your instructions?" Mr. Grimeson answered, "I'm clear." "Good," said Spartan. "Don't make us look bad. We'll talk in about two weeks to see how things are going with you. Right now, I'm headed to Florida."

That same week, Mr. Wilde had a talk with the secretary of Homeland Security. *I edited the beginning a little and it answers this question.* The two considered themselves friends, since they had gotten to know each other very well through LIFE Academy's numerous accomplishments and advancements in technology. Mr. Wilde told the secretary about the League Elite's plan to stop the importation of illegal drugs into the country. To which the secretary replied, "You do realize that stopping the importation of illegal drugs is virtually impossible, we simply fight it as best we can." "Yes, I do know how difficult of a task it has been," said Mr. Wilde. And with a voice of full assurance, he went on to say, "But the league has been working extremely hard over the past few years to create a solution that would make the 'virtually impossible' not only possible, but probable." Almost in total disbelief, the secretary responded, "Probable!" "Absolutely probable!" said Mr. Wilde. Then calming his tone a bit but still attempting to persuade, he said, "Believe me when I say this: the plan is already in motion, and with your support, the drug problem will no longer exist a year from now."

Still not convinced, the secretary asked, "Well, if the plan is already in motion, then what is it that you want from me?" "Please hear me out," said Mr. Wilde. "I cannot tell you how much your encouragement alone would boost the league's morale, knowing that the nation's Department of Homeland Security is behind and is supporting their efforts. However, as important as your moral support is, the main reason we will need your help is because you have the manpower. While it is true that our team of ten is highly trained and have taken on monumental assignments in the past that involved fighting and defeating large numbers of armed criminals, winning the battle of the borders will require many more hands than our twenty." Mr. Wilde noticed that the secretary was not sold on the idea, so he said, "I know that this is a huge risk for you, so I'll give you some time to think about it and discuss it with others. In a week or so, the league should have some information on our current progress in this war on drugs. Possibly, we can talk then. Deal?" As they shook hands, the secretary took a deep breath and responded, "Deal."

At the league headquarters, Ryan, Norris and Amy, who worked shifts to monitor the Flea, were gathering and deciphering information, while Lance and Greg were finishing up on the league's latest invention: Drug Hound, which was a mist, contained in a packet carried by officers that would be released in areas where they suspect drugs to have been used or stored. Upon release, the invisible mist will be drawn to the illegal substance and when it comes in contact with the substance, illuminate in bright orange, was only months away from being complete. Cameron and Robert were there as well. Jacquelyn was off for the week but was in town. As Wilde walked in hastily, anxious to know of any new developments from the Flea, he asked, "What do we have?" Ryan responded, "Well, we are getting some information, but it'll be up to you to determine whether or not this information is good." "Okay, go ahead, give me what you have," said Mr. Wilde. Ryan began, "First of all, we have successfully kept the Flea hidden from anyone. No one has noticed, even though we've moved about quite a bit. What's more is that everything about the Flea is working properly. We have had no sound or video problems, and we've yet to loose Mr. Grimeson's exact location." Cameron interjected, "And because everything is working properly, we now know Jeff Spartan's whereabouts as well." Making sure he had the right guy in mind, Mr. Wilde asked, "Now, Jeff Spartan, he is the number 2 guy on the East Coast, right?" "Exactly," said Cameron. "Well, it sounds like things are going better than expected," said Mr. Wilde.

In order that Mr. Wilde wouldn't get too excited, Cameron let him know of the not-so-good news. He said, "Sir, we do have to inform you of something that has us a little worried." "I'm listening," said Mr. Wilde. Cameron continued, "Well, after the camera flash in the warehouse, Mr. Grimeson became acutely aware that someone was onto him. He believes that it's one of his own who is leaking information. Therefore, a scheduled drug delivery, which was supposed to take place in a few days, has been postponed until further notice. We've missed that one and probably won't get another chance at it. However, new information has been placed on a disc that will be delivered to a person they called Dennis. It is most probable that it contains the information for another huge delivery. Now that Mr. Grimeson's conversation with Mr. Spartan has already revealed to us the exact name and address of the person who will read the disc, we really have no more use for the Flea, because Mr. Grimeson is a big risk right now. He's sort of 'out of the game' until he can figure out who is trying to get information out of him."

Being a little down about the fact that they couldn't get more information out of the Flea than they did, the room became silent, as everyone started thinking long and hard about the situation, when all of a sudden, Norris, with a bit of enthusiasm, said, "Perhaps this is the time for the Remote Info-Hog!" This is also a tiny like the flea, but it grabs and downloads information from any computer or computerized device remotely to an actual hard drive at Life league headquarters. Turning to Mr. Wilde, he said, "Sir, you know it's something that we've been waiting a long time to use." Mr. Wilde, being slightly pessimistic about the idea, said, "I understand your zeal, Norris, but there are a few major problems with using this device. The first is that it cannot copy the information directly from the disc. We have to wait until it has been opened on a computer. The second is that, just as with the Flea, the Remote Info-Hog only works at very close distances. I have no doubt that Gain can get close enough to copy the information, but I'm not so sure if he can do it without arising some suspicion. If they suspect anything, they will not go through with this delivery. This takes us to the biggest problem: security. We all know that wherever this disc is going, the place will be guarded heavily with dogs, armed men, and cameras. If we can find an answer to these problems, we can go with it. If not, we'll have to think of something else."

After everyone had quieted themselves and began to think of possible solutions, Lance, who had a secret crush on Selena and hated the fact that she and Gain were together and would be away for a few more days, made a suggestion, "I know that Gain and Selena are enjoying their much-deserved break from work, but I believe the only way we're going to find a solution is if all of the members are present." And without even a thought, everyone agreed that Selena and Gain should return immediately, and Jackie would have to come in from her time off. After Lance finished talking, Mr. Wilde, who for a while now had a haunch about Lance's feelings for Selena, walked over to him while the others continued to talk among themselves. Lance noticed the smirk on Mr. Wilde's face as he walked over and nervously asked, "What…what's the matter? Is there something wrong with me? Did I say something I should not have?" Mr. Wilde responded, "No, no, no, you're fine. I just have one question to ask." Pausing for a few seconds, he asked, "How far are you willing to go to get her?" Knowing that it would be pointless to try and play dumb, Lance lowered his head, and lifting it back up again, he said, "It's that obvious, huh?" Mr. Wilde replied, "Well, you're looking at someone who has been around young men and women for a while now. What's obvious to me may not be the least bit noticeable to your peers. So don't worry about what others may be thinking." Breathing a sigh of relief, Lance smiled and said, "Thanks. I would hate to think that others, especially Gain, knew of my feelings for Selena." Mr. Wilde concluded the discussion by saying, "We'll talk, because I really want to know how far you're willing to go."

"Mr. Wilde, I have Gain and Selena on speakerphone. Do you want to say anything to them?" asked Ryan. Mr. Wilde answered, "No, not really, just let the two lovebirds know that we're having a meeting in seventeen hours, and they are expected to be present." "You know we heard that 'lovebird' part!" said Selena. Mr. Wilde chuckled and said, "I'm just kidding, but not about the meeting. So get moving." They both responded, "We're on our way," and hung up the phone. "Let's see. That's about four days," Gain said to Selena. "I do believe that's a record," she responded. As the two began to walk back to Gain's house from the park, their conversation continued, "Yeah, maybe the next time we go somewhere together, we'll get a full five days," said Gain. "Let's hope," said Selena.

Gain and Selena had done so much together during this trip that aside from sleeping, there was hardly a time when they were not seen with one another. They were both trying to get used to the new relationship. Selena loved it but did not quite know how to respond to the very romantic Gain, who was saying everything she had ever wanted to hear from a man and doing things that made her smile instead of getting upset. Gain loved it as well but was uncertain as to how long he could keep Selena smiling. He was starting to feel the pressure to perform without spoiling the fun.

But something nearly magical happened on the third night, the night before they got the call from league headquarters. Gain and Selena had gone out to watch a movie. They were both a little nervous, but they got through it. Afterward, Gain took Selena to the park, and as she sat in a swing, He stood behind her and lightly pushed her while they talked. "Gain," said Selena, smiling and enjoying every bit of attention Gain was giving her. "Yes," said Gain. "How comfortable are you with our relationship going from strictly platonic to, well, something more than just best friends?" Selena asked. "I will admit," said Gain, "I am not as comfortable as I was a year ago, when I only thought of you as my friend, but what I feel for you now is so wonderful that it's worth being a little uncomfortable." Gain tenderly brought the swing to a halt, as Selena remained seated. Then walking in front to face her, he lowered himself and looked at her saying, "Please believe me when I say this. You have a beauty like no other woman I've encountered, and for the life of me, I do not understand how I couldn't have seen it until now. If being comfortable means losing what I feel at this very moment, I choose to remain uncomfortable. My heart…is with you." Selena smiled and softly placed her right hand on the side of Gain's face.

Gain continued, "The question now is, how comfortable are you"—emphasizing *you*—"with our new relationship?" Jokingly, Selena gave Gain a mean look, and within seconds, she put on a smallish smile because she had come up with a decent response to his question. Selena stood up, and taking Gain by the hand, she escorted him over to the car and said,

"For so long, this has been my life, figuring out how things work. I've become so good at it that I know everything there is to know about this car and any other piece of machinery. On the other hand, I've known you for about twelve years now, and we've been very good friends for almost all of those years. Yet when I look at you or even think about you, I realize that there is so much more hidden inside. I want to get to know you in every way possible." Sitting down on the hood of the car, as Gain, hanging on her every word, sat down beside her, Selena continued, "Yes, I'm also uncomfortable with going further than just friendship, because I don't want to somehow lose what we have. But if there is anything in life worth the hard work and commitment needed to make a relationship on this level work, it's you, Gain." It was on that night that the two of them saw what everyone else had seen all along: they were meant for each other.

Currently, Selena and Gain are getting ready to leave for California. "Selena, what time is our flight?" asked Gain. "The plane takes off at seven thirty, so we have to be there by six thirty to be safe. We really do not want to miss this one," said Selena. As Gain was helping Selena pack and getting everything ready to leave, his parents came into the room with worried looks on their faces. "Is there anything you guys are holding back from us?" asked Alicia. Steve added, "What's the deal with coming in for a few days and leaving out in a hurry? Is the consulting business getting so short of workers that no one is able to take a decent vacation, or is there more to you two than what you're willing to let us see?" Gain and Selena looked at each other as if they knew one day this would happen. Then Gain looked at his parents and said, "Mom,

Dad, you are going to have to trust us on this one. I know this is not what you wanted to hear, but it's all I can say right now. I assure you that we are not in trouble or anything like that, we just cannot tell you why we have to leave so sudden. Please say that you're not going to worry about us."

Steve responded, "Gain, you have to be more realistic than that. We will not stop worrying about you, especially since you're being so secretive about what's going on. You are our son, and Selena is so dear to us she's like a daughter." Steve paused and thought for a second, saying, "Nevertheless, you've always been good kids, so we know that you are even better and more responsible adults. We're going to leave you alone for now." Alicia interjected, "So there's nothing you can tell us to make us feel a little better?" Gain thought for a moment and said, "Umm…we don't…use… guns?" When she heard Gain's response, Selena began to clap, saying, "Good answer, Gain, good answer! Yes! Woo-hoo! Good answer, Gain!" Steve and Alicia started laughing, and the tension in the air was broken. "You both are psycho," said Alicia, "but we love you so much." And with that, Steve and Alicia left them to their packing.

When the packing was over and the luggage was put into the car, they all sat down, including Angela, in the family room for the remaining thirty minutes and talked about the good old days and the days to come. Angela was even bold enough to ask about a wedding date, a question to which, of course, neither Gain nor Selena had an answer. They simply said that they were going to take it slow and enjoy one another. When the time was up, they kissed and hugged and said their good-byes, and Gain and Selena left for the airport.

While Selena and Gain were on their way back to California, Mr. Wilde had Lance over for dinner. It was quiet, but not because they were both enjoying their food too much to talk. It was that Lance felt a little uneasy. So Mr. Wilde spoke first, "What's wrong, Lance?" he said. "You haven't eaten much of your meal. Are you not too fond of seafood?" Lance responded, "No, that's not it. I actually love seafood. The meal is awesome, and if my belly weren't so full of butterflies, my plate would be empty." Mr. Wilde chuckled, saying, "Lance, you have the butterflies! But you've been here before, a few times actually." Lance said, "I know, but I'm not nervous because I'm eating dinner at my boss's house. I'm just caught between feelings. I've been thinking about the question you asked me: how far am I willing to go to get Selena. To be honest, Mr. Wilde, one part of me feels that it will be wrong to try and get in between her relationship with Gain. However, there's another part of me that says Selena will be better off getting to know me, intimately."

Now, to say that Mr. Wilde was a man of great influence would be a huge understatement. The fact is, he could do and say almost anything he wanted to suit his purposes and would never be challenged the least bit. People trusted him because through the LIFE Academy, Life League, and League Elite, so much good had been done in the world. However, what nobody knew, except a few members of Life League, was that for the past twenty-five years, Edward Wilde, in his quest to rid the United States of its social problems, would periodically use his credibility to cause those who stood in his way to "disappear." Some would be set up and charged with criminal activity, others would be bribed and or blackmailed, and for a few, it was worse.

Even though Gain was a much-needed addition to the League Elite team, Mr. Wilde knew that Gain's ability to detect when something is wrong, out of place, or dangerous might pose a problem to his plan. It is true, Mr. Wilde desired to make America a better place socially, but the means by which this would happen was not what most would call honorable. The truth is, Mr. Wilde's plan to rid the United States of its social problems was through massive, widespread euthanasia. His fear was that as things went along, Gain would somehow pick up on what was going on and attempt to expose the plan. Years back, someone tried to expose Mr. Wilde's plan and had to pay dearly. Mr. Wilde already had enough support from the Life League and was quite certain that, providing they got the drug bust, he could deceive the secretary of Homeland Defense into providing workers to do the legwork. He'd worked too hard, too long, and had come too far to allow one man to end it all. Gain had to go.

Back at the dinner table, Mr. Wilde continued to talk to Lance. "I understand your dilemma, Lance, but I believe that in life we only get a few opportunities to do what makes us the happiest. If we miss those chances at true happiness and fulfillment, we have to settle for whatever is left." Elevating his tone and speaking with a sense of conviction and frustration, Mr. Wilde said, "Gain is an unstable man! He's simply a glorified daredevil! One day, someone's going to catch him and take him out. Then Selena will be left all alone. Why put her through the unnecessary pain? Just consider her single and available right now and pursue your desires. Think of Gain as an obstacle that must be removed. If you let him remain, I think you will have missed out on a major part of your true happiness."

Still contemplating, Lance asked, "So what is it that I can do to, as you say, 'remove this obstacle'?" "You must do whatever must be done. It's not the method that is so important, but the will to follow through. I'll ask you once more. How far are you willing to go to have Selena as your close companion?" Lance lowered his head and closed his eyes, as if praying, then he lifted slowly and looked Mr. Wilde directly in the eyes and said, "All the way." Mr. Wilde stood up, walked over to Lance's chair, placed his hand on his shoulder, and said, "That's exactly what I've been waiting to hear. You are only weeks, maybe days, away from getting your reward."

That evening, Mr. Wilde began to share with Lance a bit of false information about Gain. He told him that for the past six months, the Life League, along with the FBI, had been secretly investigating Gain's activities on suspicions of illegal purchasing and selling of firearms. "Do you know that all of the Elite members' homes are equipped with the best security systems around?" asked Mr. Wilde. "Why, of course, I do. I helped to invent them, remember?" said Lance. "So then you must know what my next statement will be?" Lance paused for a second, took a deep breath in and out, and said reluctantly, "You want me to disarm the system." Mr. Wilde smiled. "For how long do you want it disarmed?" Lance asked. "For a long-enough period of time so that someone can get in and look around while he's not there," said Mr. Wilde, and as he prepared to let Lance go home for the night, he said, "I'll keep you posted. Stay on the alert." "Sure thing," said Lance. "See you tomorrow morning."

The Perfect Plan

The next day, the meeting began at five o'clock in the morning. All were present and made it there on time. Gain and Selena were a little bit tired from the five-and-a-half-hour flight and had no real time to recover. Nevertheless, everyone was alert and anxious to get started. "Good morning to you all," said Mr. Wilde. "Welcome back, Selena, welcome back, Gain." The two answered, "Thank you, sir." Mr. Wilde continued, "As most of you know, we have stumbled upon a delicate situation. Therefore, much of what I'm going say in the next couple of minutes is mainly for Gain, Selena, and Jacquelyn. We have obtained a wealth of information, thanks to the Flea, but because of suspicion about the camera flash, Mr. Grimeson will soon cease all of his drug-related activities. So obviously, our uses of the Flea, as awesome an invention as it is, are relatively over. However, all is not quite lost. Mr. Grimeson has one more duty before he goes on vacation for a while. He has to deliver a disc containing information of a formulating drug delivery. From now until noon, I want you to break yourselves up into three groups and figure out how to get a copy of what's on that disc without arousing any thoughts of foul play. We cannot afford to lose what we have."

Immediately, they all broke up into groups and started brainstorming, and after about five hours of thinking, debating, suggesting, and compromising, Lance came up with an idea that would most likely work. His suggestion was that one of the members would have to become Mr. Grimeson. They would use the video from the Flea to duplicate his features, voice, and mannerisms. For Greg and Lance, it would take no time at all to get the mask and hair together. After telling Mr. Wilde of the plan, he couldn't believe that he didn't think of it first. Everyone was excited about the prospect of getting another chance, so everyone worked hard to formulate a plan. After a couple more hours of thinking, the group figured out the perfect strategy. They knew that Mr. Grimeson was already wanted by the FBI for numerous drug-distribution charges, but he was very elusive. All they had to work with were a few old sketches. Nonetheless, it was those same old sketches that Norris and Cameron, a.k.a. the "Hound Dogs," used to track Mr. Grimeson down, though he'd always been good at disguising himself. Only the League Elite knew his whereabouts and every move. Therefore, they decided to inform the FBI of their plan.

That same hour, Special Agent Peters was invited to the league headquarters. He could not believe what he was seeing actual, live-action footage of Floyd Grimeson, compliments of the Flea. Agent Peters was so awestruck that he asked several times if it were really him. "It's him," said Ryan, "but he's only bait right now. We have to wait until a specified time before you guys can go in and arrest him. Also, you'll have to take him with very minimal attraction." "We know our jobs," said agent Peters, "but are you sure he won't get away if we keep waiting around? How do you know this Flea will not fail or be discovered somehow?" Slightly disturbed by his lack of faith in the league's abilities, Mr. Wilde interjected, "Agent Peters, you must know that our inventions are known for their high quality in design. If the Flea was going to fail, it would have done so during the testing phase. Now, as for Mr. Grimeson discovering that he's being monitored, there is virtually no possibility of this occurring. Ryan and his team are very careful not to let that happen." Quite humbled by Mr. Wilde's words, Agent Peters responded, "Sorry for questioning you, sir. You guys found him, so I'll follow your lead."

Being that it was only Thursday, the League Elite and the FBI had at least two days to get everything lined up and ready for execution. By Saturday morning, everything was in order. The only question was who would wear the disguise and essentially become Mr. Grimeson. It did not take long for everyone to agree that Gain should do it since he had become so accustomed to putting himself in dangerous situations and coming out fine. So he busied himself with learning how to be Mr. Grimeson. Gain was a little bit smaller, so he had to get some extra padding, but everything else was fine. This assignment required virtually no talking, so Gain did not have to worry too much about altering his voice.

When Sunday morning had come, four FBI agents were positioned at the airport, just beyond the security gates. As the clueless Mr. Grimeson cleared the metal detectors, the agents rushed in, grabbed him, handcuffed him, and took him quickly to a room where they found the package containing the disc. They also took his boarding pass. Mr. Grimeson put up a little fight, but the agents were too strong to overpower. "What are you doing to me? I haven't done anything wrong!" said Mr. Grimeson. "Oh, we beg to differ, Mr. Grimeson," said Agent Peters, who walked in the room just as Mr. Grimeson finished his statement. Agent Peters continued, "You are Floyd Grimeson, or are you?" Just then, Gain, disguised as Mr. Grimeson, walked into the room and said, "No, I'm Floyd Grimeson. Do you have my disc?" Agent Peters took the disc and boarding pass from one of the other agents and handed them over to Gain. As Gain left out to prepare to board the plane, Mr. Grimeson yelled, "You'll never get away with this!"

Gain only had a few minutes before boarding call, but he knew he had to copy the disc to his laptop before he got on the plane. The team had already recreated the package. Everything, including the writing, was exactly like the original box. Therefore, Gain did not have to worry about resealing the package. After removing the disc from the package, Gain copied it to his computer and placed all the contents of the package into the new box. He then e-mailed the information from the disc to Ryan at the headquarters. Once he received confirmation from Ryan that everything was fine, Gain was set for phase two, but prior to boarding the plane, he left all of his belongings, including his laptop, to one of the agents. All he took with him was a briefcase containing only the package to be delivered and his boarding pass. Having no gadgets or weapons, Gain boarded the plane as Mr. Grimeson.

Back at the headquarters, Ryan had already downloaded and opened the file. The information was encrypted, but for

Ryan and Norris, files presented in plain text were not worth reading; they needed a challenge. Needless to say, they broke the code within minutes. As Mr. Wilde stood behind them, they began to convert the data. Reading the information, they found that there was definitely a huge delivery on its way scheduled for the following Sunday. Mr. Wilde spoke saying, "Guys, this is good. This is a monumental opportunity for us all. Hard work, no doubt, pays off." The disc revealed that Glenn Figel, the CEO of Bunch-a-Barks Dog Food Inc., plans to use five ships to bring in one hundred tons of cocaine in order to start up a new distribution center. They've informed the port authorities of the huge shipment, telling them that the reason for the shipment is for the opening of Bunch-a-Barks' new warehouse and that the ships are loaded with dog food. Everything was right there on the disc: the times, the drop-off points, the number of trucks needed as well as personnel; nothing was left out.

Back at the league headquarters, since Gain was away and would be for at least eight more hours and everybody else was sort of stuck there until more news surfaced, Lance decided to have a little talk with Selena. "Sorry you and Gain had to come back so soon," he said. "Well, we've sort of gotten used to it now. It's the nature of our jobs," answered Selena. "That's true," said Lance as he continued to ask questions, "So how did it go?" Selena, a little hesitant to talk anymore, asked, "How did what go?" "You know," said Lance, "being with Gain." Selena, being totally disturbed by Lance's presence, responded, "Oh, I'm sorry, Lance, your questions are getting a bit too personal. I'm going to go work on something. I'll talk to you later." Mumbling to himself, Lance said, "Wow, Lance, you sure are smooth." Sadly, with head hanging down, he walked over to his station to work.

As the morning went on, all was going just as planned. Gain was having no problems at all. He had already reached St. Louis, rented a car, and was on the way to Dennis's house. Arriving at the gate on time, Gain was asked by one of the guards to step out of the vehicle. When he stepped out of the car, he was searched and the car was searched thoroughly. The whole process took about thirty minutes, but Gain held his composure. At the end of the search, Gain was allowed to drive into the complex. He got to the front door and said the password when asked. Five minutes later, Dennis came to the front door, where they exchanged possessions as planned. Finally, after leaving Dennis's place, Gain delivered the money to the guys at the dog-food warehouse and headed back to the airport. One week later, as scheduled, the delivery was made, and as soon as the ships reached the ports, they were all seized and searched. All one hundred tons were recovered, and fifty people were arrested. Many, including Bunch-a-Barks' CEO, went into hiding until they could figure out what to do about their losses. Later they would put together another delivery that was not foiled by the Life League. Nevertheless, this bust would get the attention of the right people; those who would help Mr. Wilde to get his plan under way.

The day after the seizure, Mr. Wilde returned to the office of the secretary of Homeland Defense. The secretary had been present at the drug bust and could not believe how much cocaine was headed for the streets of the America at one time. However, rather than being excited about the confiscation, the secretary was disturbed by the fact that at any time, someone else could try the same thing and no one would be able to stop it. As soon as Mr. Wilde walked into the office, the secretary, a little discouraged, started talking, "Ed, we don't have enough ports, enough people, or enough time to stop and thoroughly search every ship that sails onto the shores of America. I sure hope that you have something more than just checking ships. Even if we did somehow lessen the amount of drugs shipped in, we still have to deal with the stuff that's made here in our own country!"

Shocked at what he was hearing, Mr. Wilde responded, "I take it you were not impressed with our help?" Apologetically, the secretary answered, "No, it's not that. To be honest with you, I never knew it was possible to seize such a large quantity of pure cocaine. You and your team, you guys are absolutely amazing. I only wish we had about one hundred more teams just like yours spread all over the United States. But you do realize that this will not discourage these dealers from shipping drugs to make money. They'll just be a lot more careful next time."

Just then, Mr. Wilde asked the secretary if he could spare a few more minutes. The secretary replied, "Sure, I've been waiting to see what the league has been working on." Mr. Wilde opened his briefcase and took out a puck-sized flat metal canister and handed it to the secretary. "What's this?" asked the secretary. "That, my dear friend, is what we call the Drug Hound, the answer to the nationwide drug problem," said Mr. Wilde. Looking down at the canister, somewhat chuckling, the secretary said, "Ed, you know I've always been one who will always call it like I see it, and I'm never really bothered by offending anyone with the words I say. Are you sure you want to put yourself through this?" Mr. Wilde responded, "You may have tough words, but I have tough skin and the determination of a pit bull. When I believe in something enough, nothing, especially not criticism, will stop me from getting exactly what I want!" Removing the canister from the secretary's hand, Mr. Wilde continued, "I am fed up with the drug problem, and I believe this is a positive step in the direction of reaching my goal! If you'd like, I can go somewhere else and try another route."

Not wanting to create any bad relations with Mr. Wilde, the secretary said, "That will not be necessary, Ed. Maybe I just need to hear a little bit about it before I make any judgment calls." Mr. Wilde's tone changed drastically. He became excited as ever about the opportunity to explain the plan to the secretary. He said that the canister was simply one of the thirty-eight thousand that will be placed one hundred miles apart throughout the United States, including Alaska and Hawaii. The canisters, after activation, would be self-sustaining. They become active at the presence of cocaine within a fifty-mile radius of each canister. Upon activation and within seconds, invisible vapors will be emitted. "These vapors," said Mr. Wilde, "are harmless to any organism, but when they come in contact with cocaine, they immediately neutralize the active ingredient while creating after ingestion a substance that permanently rejects future ingestion of cocaine." The secretary looked a little confused, so Mr. Wilde said, "In other words, these canisters will rid all of the cocaine and crack addicts of the desire for these drugs. Once we eliminate the use, we eliminate the demand. When the demand is gone, well, you know where I'm going."

The secretary was as impressed with the idea alone as he was with the prospect of living in a cocaine-free nation. He then asked Mr. Wilde if he had any plans for other drugs. Mr. Wilde answered, "We do, but let's take our time, shall we?" They both laughed. Standing up and gathering his material for his next meeting, the secretary said, "Well, Ed, I cannot come up with any constructive criticism right now. In fact, I'm almost ready to pose this idea to the president and all the other important signers needed to get this operation up and running. Can we meet again one week from today?" Mr. Wilde said, "We sure can, and in our next meeting, I'll let you know all of the details of the plan. I'll also bring one of the guys responsible for this invention." "That will be fine," said the secretary, "and I'll try to have a few more important people here as well." With that, they shook hands, and Mr. Wilde left the office.

EVIL ED

Over the next few days, things had slowed down around town. It was almost as if the big drug bust had most of the criminals living in fear. It was also slow at the league headquarters. Everyone had gone back to their regular jobs except for Lance and Greg, who were finalizing the details of the Drug Hound. This was perfect timing for Gain and Selena to hang out and have fun in their newfound relationship. That Friday, Gain and Selena went out on a date that they had planned earlier that same week. They went to a nice restaurant where they ate, listened to music, and even danced. They thoroughly enjoyed one another so much that Gain decided to take her for a late-night walk on the beach.

As they walked and held hands, Gain began to open up to Selena. He asked, "Have you ever thought about what life would be like if you were not a part of the League Elite?" A bit surprised by the question, Selena answered, "Yes, I have, but why are you asking this question?" Looking up at the sky, Gain said, "I just don't think I can do this anymore." Turning toward Selena, he continued, "The last couple of weeks with you have been incredible, almost unreal. I had no clue that I could feel the way I do for you. I know this sounds funny, but I can see clearly now, the rain is gone…" Selena did laugh, but she quickly regained her composure, knowing that Gain was serious and on a roll. So she put her arm around his and said, "I'm sorry, Gain, you can keep singing. I mean…" She started laughing again, but harder this time. As she fell to the ground, she said while still laughing, "Gain, I was not ready for…" Selena's laughing slowed, as she watched Gain silently sit down beside her and gaze out into the ocean. "I take it you're not in a laughing mood, huh?" she said to Gain, rubbing him on his back. "No, I am. That was funny, Selena, it really was," Gain said in a nonhumorous voice, still looking at the water.

By now, Selena had become a little concerned, so she took hold of Gain's chin and turned his head, looking him directly in the eyes, and with a serious voice said, "Now you're being funny." "I was just thinking," said Gain. "What would have happened if while I was delivering the disc to that guy, Dennis, something went terribly wrong? What if they would have found me out? I know for sure that I would not be here with you." Standing up and walking toward the water, Gain continued to talk, "Selena, I never used to have thoughts like this. I just did what I felt needed to be done. Now I realize, because I've fallen absolutely in love with you, I have to put a lot more thought to the things I do, because I do not want what we have to end ever."

Selena was touched by Gain's words but wasn't quite sure if he was simply speaking in the moment or if he was talking about commitment. She stood up and held onto his arm again, resting her head on his shoulder. Then looking up toward him she asked, "How can you be certain that what you feel right now is real?" Gain answered, It's because you're real, Selena, what you just did is proof of your realness." Turning toward her, he continued, "I was in the moment, right, and when I said something that struck you as corny, you laughed and called me on it. And even though your timing was off, you didn't shy away, get defensive, or become uncomfortable. You remained cool and continued to talk to me. You're not afraid to be yourself, and that's what helps me to be myself."

Satisfied with Gain's answer, Selena then asked. "So are you saying that you are no longer going to be a part of the League Elite team?" "That's what I'm saying, but I'm going to give it a couple of months before I let Mr. Wilde know," said Gain. He continued, "Selena, I honestly like how I'm feeling right now. It seems as though I'm letting go of a huge weight and actually starting to live." Smiling, Selena asked, "You feel that way because of me?" "Only because of you," said Gain. The two continued to hold hands as they walked back to the car. It was already past 12:00 a.m., so as Gain was driving Selena home, she fell asleep in the car. Arriving at her house, Gain carried her to the doorstep and stood her upright. Waking up, Selena was surprised that Gain had carried her so far without her knowing it. Nonetheless, she was happy he did it. As he was about to leave, he took Selena's keys and opened the door for her. He noticed that she was smiling, so he paused for a moment and silently smiled back. "Gain," said Selena, "you're an awesome guy, you know that?" Gain's knees almost buckled as he said, "Thanks, Selena, you're an awesome girl." "Good night," said Selena. "Good night," said Gain, then he walked back to his car and drove home.

Being somewhat close to Mr. Wilde, Gain let him know that he and Selena would be hanging out together and would be out of the house on Friday evening. Therefore, Mr. Wilde contacted Lance and told him that Friday night would be the time to shut off Gain's alarm. Lance, believing what Mr. Wilde had said to him, that Gain had been seriously involved in a federal offense, told Mr. Wilde, that he would make sure to let him know when it was safe to enter Gain's home. In the mean time, Mr. Wilde informed Lance of the change in plans; that is, rather than just look around, he was going to have someone plant a tracking device in Gain's wallet. Therefore, Lance knew that he was in for a long night, being that Gain would probably not be home until late.

At around eight o'clock on Friday night, Lance called Gain's home from a pay phone, and since there was no answer, he knew that Gain had left for the evening. That very moment, Lance shut off Gain's alarm and called Mr. Wilde, who was pleased to hear Lance's voice so soon. He had already hired a man, whom he called Terrance, to enter Gain's home at the appointed time. Mr. Wilde's instructions were for Terrance to break into Gain's home somehow, without showing signs of forced entry, and hide himself until Gain returned home and fell asleep. While Gain was sleeping, Terrance was to put the tracking device inside Gain's wallet. This device would keep track of Gain's conversations as well as his locations. After Terrance returned to Mr. Wilde, he would receive payment for his services.

It was unfortunate for Gain that one of his windows was left unlocked, because as Terrance searched for a way to get into Gain's house, he found the window, entered Gain's home, and hid himself in Gain's bedroom closet, holding a knife in his hand was just in case Gain found him, he may have to use it to get away... Terrance had further instructions to alert Mr. Wilde when he had gotten into his hiding spot and was away from the downstairs sensors. This was so that Mr. Wilde could let Lance know to remove the override of Gain's alarm system. Therefore, when Gain returned home, his system would be armed, and nothing would seem strange. Prior to leaving Gain's residence after the tracking device had been planted, Terrance would alert Mr. Wilde once more, so that Lance could override the system, enabling Terrance to leave out the front door. After a span of two minutes, Lance would rearm the system.

Gain arrived home at around one o'clock on Saturday morning. He was still thinking about Selena and the decision to leave the League Elite but was mentally and physically exhausted. He entered the house and disarmed the system as usual, but as he began to walk upstairs to his room, he felt like something was wrong. So he turned around and searched downstairs for anything out of place but found nothing. Then he armed the system and went upstairs for the night. However, he continued to feel as though something was wrong, so as he went upstairs, he checked the guestroom, bathroom, and hallway closet, still finding nothing. Yet having this feeling, he concluded that something must be in his room, so he walked in very cautiously, turned on the light, and began to look around. First, he checked behind his curtains. Terrance began to get nervous, so he readied his knife for a confrontation. Then Gain checked his covers and underneath his bed. The only place left to check was his closet. Gain now became nervous as the feeling became stronger than ever. He knew that once he opened the closet, something bad was going to happen, so he prepared himself for the worst. Finally, he took a deep breath in and out, grabbed the handle to the closet door.

By now, Terrance had positioned himself directly in front of the closet, so that when Gain opened the door, he would lunge out quickly and do whatever was necessary to escape. Just then, as Gain was about to open the door, the phone rang. Immediately, Gain released the door handle, walked over to the phone, and answered it, still keeping his eyes on the door. "Hello," he said. It was Selena. She told him that she was thinking about him too much to go to sleep, so she gave him a call. Right away, he sat down on his bed and started talking. He remained cautious for the first couple of minutes of the conversation, but after a while, he calmed himself, laid back in the bed, and forgot about the closet. Selena and Gain talked on the phone for an hour and a half. Gain had become so sleepy that twice, while talking to Selena, his words became gibberish. Finally, Selena, who was also tired, said good night. Gain responded with the same courtesy, and the two hung up their phones. Gain was no longer thinking about the closet, only about sleep. So he made himself comfortable by removing his wallet, keys, and everything else from his pockets. Then he turned off the lights, slid under the covers, and fell into a deep sleep.

As the night went on, Terrance too had become sleepy, especially from listening to Gain and Selena's conversation. So he also fell asleep in the closet but woke himself around 3:30 a.m. Carefully opening the door, Terrance was happy to find that the room had a little bit of light shining into it from the hallway. He stepped out of the closet, crept over to Gain's nightstand, and put the tracking device inside one of the pockets in Gain's wallet. He slowly walked out of the room and quietly alerted Mr. Wilde. Everything afterward followed as planned.

As was mentioned, Mr. Wilde was a very influential and well-respected man. There were people who would do anything for him, regardless of consequences, as long as it served to satisfy Mr. Wilde's desires. These were the people whom he would turn to in order to cause massive chaos in Gain's life. He started by sending out e-mails to twenty different people, whom he knew would literally die for him. The e-mail was a special invitation to a meeting at his house. No one from the Life League or the League Elite was invited.

Three days after the tracking device was planted, the meeting convened. At the meeting, he gave each one of them a monitor for Gain's tracking device. He then told them that he wanted two teams of ten. One team would be responsible for ruining Gain's relationship with Selena, and the other team would follow by ending Gain's life. Mr. Wilde figured that Gain's defenses would be weakened after he had lost the love of his life. Therefore, it was important for the second team to wait until Selena had decided to end her relationship with Gain before they would attempt to harm him. He stressed that there could be no evidence of foul play. The team would have to make Gain's death seem as though it were accidental. The meeting adjourned, and the two teams, eager to please Mr. Wilde, awaited further orders.

Prior to giving Team One the go ahead, Mr. Wilde had to make sure that his plans for the Drug Hound were going to be accepted by the secretary of Homeland Security, so a day after the private meeting, he and Lance had a meeting with the secretary, who also invited the secretary of State and a few other high-profile individuals. On the way to the meeting, Mr. Wilde thanked Lance for his assistance and assured him that he was doing the right thing. Also, he told him to prepare himself for an intimate conversation with Selena. Eager to hear something positive about Selena, Lance asked, "So she wants to talk to me?" Mr. Wilde responded, "Slow down, Lance. I'm only saying that I remember what we discussed in regard to your desire to have her in your life. You did your part, now it's time for me to do mine. The rest, well, the rest is up to you. Whether she wants to continue to talk to you or not, that will depend on how well you communicate your feelings. If all goes well today, you should begin to notice a different Selena in just a few days. I'll tell you when you should call her." "Wow," said Lance, "this is definitely good news to me. May I ask how you're going to get this done?" Mr. Wilde, getting a little bothered by Lance's questions and lack of patience, said, "Lance, if you're going to be worried about the details, I'm inclined to think that you may not want her as much as you say. Now, do you want me to go forward or not?" Lance answered, "I do." Mr. Wilde ended the conversation by saying, "Well, you are going to have to trust me on this one."

When they arrived at the secretary's office, Mr. Wilde, along with Lance, put on a wonderful presentation of what the Drug Hound would do for the country. Everyone was impressed, but one of the members present asked, "So what do we do about the need for jobs and the poverty issue that will arise when that huge amount of money that illegal drug distribution brings into this country is gone? Also, what happens when the cocaine and crack addicts turn to something else like heroin?" Mr. Wilde responded, "I thank you for that insightful question, and I do have a legitimate solution."

As he stood up and walked around the room as if addressing a class, he continued, "First of all, we must agree that the Drug Hound, when put in operation, will get rid of the huge cocaine problem. That alone is worth the investment. But to answer your question, what we can do in the next six months is create jobs that will suit the needs of those who will no longer have drugs as a means of income. One suggestion I have is to use any money that we no longer have to spend on the efforts to end cocaine distribution to build and develop rehabilitation centers. These will not be jails, but actual, functional centers with the purpose of taking ex-drug addicts and ex-drug dealers from being dependent on cocaine to being totally independent, hardworking citizens."

"What will make these centers any different from the treatment centers we have now?" asked the secretary of Homeland Security. "The difference," said Mr. Wilde, "will be in our approach to opening these new centers. Instead of just building them, opening them, and then trying to persuade people to come, we will start campaigning for the centers months before they even open."

Becoming passionate about his speech, Mr. Wilde began to elevate his voice a bit as he said, "It's time for this nation to really declare war on illegal drugs, not just play games! There are too many families that know firsthand how much pain cocaine and other drugs can bring into the lives of good people. Let's get Americans excited about ending the cocaine problem for good. We should get everyone involved. Ministers should be preaching about the end of the cocaine era from their pulpits. Instead of schools telling kids to 'just say no', they should be telling them to 'just say no more!' This is not an impossible task by any means." Mr. Wilde quieted his voice some as he said, "If we get enough people excited about ending the drug problem for good, the centers will be successful, and jobs won't be an issue because everyone will be working toward the same goal. Within five years, we plan on having the same type of system in place for heroin, meth, ecstasy, opium, and any other illegal drug that plagues this country. We believe it all starts right here. The decision is yours gentlemen. Are you with us?

As Mr. Wilde took his seat, the secretary of state spoke, saying, "Let's say we decide to go with this plan, what exactly will you need from us?" Mr. Wilde responded, "Simple manpower is all we will need, that and your trust in our abilities. However, if you can't fully trust us yet, we'll take the workers. I'll let Lance give the details. Lance."

Lance started by unraveling a very large map of the United States that was covered with red dots. He placed the map in the center of the table and began to explain, "As you can see, this is a United States map, and you've probably figured that each one of these red dots represents one Drug Hound canister. If that is what you thought, then you've figured correctly. However, what you probably do not know is that every one of these spots is already marked and ready for the canisters to be attached. All we need is the personnel to place the canisters in every one of these spots." Lance continued, "The way this system works is through a wireless series connection, meaning, though there are no need for wires, each canister depends on the other in order to operate. We've chosen series rather than parallel, mainly because we want to wait until every canister is in place before operation begins. Since this will be a nationwide campaign, we want everyone to work on their individual parts as though others depend on them."

Over the next thirty minutes, Lance explained how each canister should be placed between two and four feet underground and that if any canister was disturbed after activation, it would set off an alarm. He also let them know that none of the marked areas were on private property or underwater, but that there were no "cold spots" where cocaine would go undetected. The entire country would be covered. Before concluding his talk, he reemphasized that the canisters were tested over and over, none of them having been found the least bit harmful to any living organism. "In fact," said Lance, "over the last five years, we've been working on getting it FDA approved, and just three months ago, we got it approved and suitable for use." Everyone in the room became extremely excited about the plan, and they were all anxious to get started.

"Mr. Wilde, Lance," said the secretary of Homeland Security, "we thank you for opening our eyes to this wonderful opportunity to make things better in our country. I would never have thought that this would happen in my lifetime. You have our full support. However, before we can provide any physical help, we must get confirmation that it is approved by the FDA. When we get that information, we will contact you and begin operations immediately." Smiling,

Mr. Wilde said, "We're looking forward to it," as he and Lance departed the room.

No one had a clue, not even Lance, that Mr. Wilde had already contaminated these canisters. They were no longer harmless to living organisms but were set to kill within three days anyone who had the presence of cocaine in their bodies. Mr. Wilde knew that there was no way he would be able to escape the blame for such a disaster, so he and four other members of the Life League who were also in on Mr. Wilde's plan purchased one-way tickets to another country where no one would ever find them. They would leave on the day when the canisters were set to be activated; they were hoping within six months.

Mr. Wilde had not always been such an evil man. He began to change when he saw how drugs were not only destroying the lives of the reckless and depressed. It was almost thirty years ago when he witnessed one of the LIFE Academy graduates die because of an overdose on drugs. In that same year, three more of his graduates, whom he cared for dearly, were found to be heavily addicted to cocaine. It was then that Mr. Wilde began an honest attempt to rid the country of this life-destroying drug. However, as the years passed and the amount of drug abusers increased, he started to notice that the users were committing more and more crimes and ruining more and more lives. Therefore, Mr. Wilde finally concluded that the problem was not the cocaine itself, but the users of cocaine. That very moment, he developed a hatred for every drug addict, especially cocaine addicts, on the face of the earth. In his opinion, drug users were walking, talking dead men and women who could only do one main thing: destroy the lives of others.

Presently, Mr. Wilde and his four friends are making sure that every tie to the contamination on the canisters is connected to Lance, who is totally in the dark. Mr. Wilde kept Lance so busy that it was nothing for him to get Lance to sign forms that would eventually incriminate him. Lance trusted Mr. Wilde with his life. He had always viewed and respected him as a father; most of the LIFE graduates did.

Please Stop the Pain!

One week later, the secretary of Homeland Security gave Mr. Wilde a call to inform him that everything checked out right and that he was able to offer one hundred people per state. This he would do without compromising any of the day-to-day operations. Mr. Wilde was pleased and started to believe that the job could be done in much less time than he had anticipated. The secretary also told him that he would talk with the president in regard to letting the nation know about what is about to happen and how everyone can help. Everything was going as well as possible for Mr. Wilde. That evening, Mr. Wilde called the members of team one and let them know that they are free to begin their work on Gain and Selena.

    Gain, still unaware of the device in his wallet, gave Selena a call after work. "Hello," said Selena. "Hi," said Gain, "How was work?" "Eh, so-so," said Selena, "I know you said that you're ready to leave the League Elite, but I'm kind of bored with my job right now. I wonder when we're going to get called in to do something adventurous and slightly dangerous." Gain laughed a little and said, "Adventurous? Slightly dangerous? Wow, you really are bored with work, aren't you? I hope that doesn't mean you're getting bored of me too." Selena, hesitant to speak, said, "Well, maybe just a little. But I think it's because we haven't done anything yet." Gain asked, "Done anything like what?" "Oh, come on, Gain!" said Selena. "You know what I mean." Chuckling, Gain said, "Yeah, you're right. I do know what you mean, and I'm ready to do something about it, but you'll have to wait until this Friday night." Selena became a little excited but then felt a little guilty and said, "Are you sure you want to do this? I don't want to pressure you or anything." Gain answered, "I'm definitely ready. I just didn't want to rush you." "Ha-ha, mister funny man, you are quite the comedian," said Selena. They both laughed a bit. "We'll talk later, okay?" said Gain. Selena answered, "Okay," and they hung up the phones.

On Thursday night, Selena and Gain talked again and made plans for their date the next day. They both agreed that they should get started early, so they planned to just meet each other at the arcade right after work. Selena had been bugging Gain about doing some of the things they used to do when they were just friends, but Gain was enjoying the walks and talks and holding hands so much that he continued to dismiss her requests. On Friday, however, Selena would get her wish granted. They had a full evening planned. They would start off at the arcade and play games until they got tired. Then they would move on to go-kart racing for an hour or so. Later they would go and play one-on-one basketball and finally get something to eat, going home dead tired. Team One heard the conversation, and by the time Gain left his job on Friday, they had formulated a plan that would cause Gain to miss the entire evening with Selena.

Gain was traveling in his car to the arcade, which was about thirty minutes from his job, when seemingly out of the blue, a police officer started following him with flashing lights and sirens. Then thinking that maybe something was wrong with his taillight, Gain pulled over. When the officers, who were really Team One members disguised as police, came up to Gain's window, they immediately told him to step out of the car and put his hands behind his head. This they did with their guns pointed toward him. Gain did exactly as they said without saying a word. He was waiting for them to say why he was pulled over. After searching him one, said, "Are you aware that there are eyewitnesses, five miles back, who say that you were the cause of an accident?" Gain answered, "No, officer, I don't remember any near accidental encounter with a car." Well," said the other, "we're going to have to take you in, because one of the people involved in the accident looks to be in pretty bad shape. Maybe the witnesses will help you to remember."

Gain knew that something weird was going on but elected to wait until he got to the police station to ask any questions. Not noticing that his cell phone and keys were taken during the search, Gain got into the back of the police car. He sat in the back for about fifteen minutes thinking about Selena and how he would explain everything to her when they arrived at the station. Then he noticed that they were leaving town. He started banging on the barrier in front of him to get their attention, but they ignored him. It was then that he knew he was being kidnapped. He tried to open the doors, but they were safety-locked. Knowing that it would be too dangerous to try and escape by breaking the windows, Gain calmed himself and decided to wait until the car stopped. An hour later, they stopped the car, got out, unlocked the doors for Gain to get out, and quickly jumped into another car that had been following them. Before Gain could get out and catch up with them, they were already gone. He was stuck in the middle of nowhere. The members of team were very clever; they did not want to risk anyone seeing Gain's car on the side of the road, so right after the fake police officers drove Gain away, someone else from the team showed up and drove his car to a less conspicuous location.

Sure enough, after Selena had waited at the arcade for forty-five minutes, not being able to contact him by any means, she decided to drive the path that Gain would take from work to the arcade to see if he had been in an accident. After she drove the path and saw nothing, Selena was both worried and upset, so she decided to go back to the arcade and play a few games to try and keep her mind from thinking the worst. After about an hour, she went home.

By now, it was getting pretty dark outside. At the point where Gain was dropped off, he was about sixty miles away from where his car was left. He had no choice but to try and walk back. He knew that he was only about five miles from a pay phone, so in his eyes, all was not lost. Gain had only walked for about fifteen minutes when a car with a middle-aged woman in it pulled up. Her car smelled strongly of perfume, because in the passenger's seat, a puddle of White Diamonds was drying. When she stopped, Gain was amazed and extremely happy that someone had actually stopped to pick him up. For some reason, this woman did not feel threatened by Gain, so when he said how far he had to go, she said that she'd have no problems taking him; however, she never warned him about the perfume. Gain's mind had become so intent on getting to his car as fast as he could that he disregarded the perfume as well as the payphones and asked the woman if she could drive as fast as she could into town. The woman replied, "I'll do my best."

Just before they got to where Gain's car was supposed to be, Gain heard the woman making a phone call to someone, saying that she was only a few minutes away. For some reason, and only for a brief moment, Gain thought about the woman's phone call and to whom she might be talking. Then as quickly as the thought came, it vanished out of his mind. Five minutes after her call, they were at Gain's car, and it was just where he had left it; the keys and cell phone were there. It was as if no one had even noticed the car. Ecstatic, to say the least, Gain thanked the woman and offered to pay her, but she refused and said, "It was my pleasure." She drove off, and Gain jumped into his car. He immediately called Selena, who had been home only for a few minutes; nevertheless, she was not in a happy mood. "Hello, Gain," said Selena. "Yes, it's me," said Gain. Selena raised her voice a tad, "Where are you? I've been so worried and mad. What happened to you?" Gain said, "It's a long story. Is it okay if I come over?" Selena sighed and said in as unenthusiastic a voice as ever, "That will be fine." Gain, sensing her disappointment, said, "Thanks, Selena. I will make it up to you. I'll be there in about twenty minutes." They exchanged good-byes and hung up their phones.

When Gain arrived at Selena's door and rang the doorbell, Selena had begun to calm herself. She was willing to take any good excuse why he did not show up. However, as soon as she opened the door, her anger rekindled. In a demanding voice, Selena asked, "Gain, who were you with?" Taken aback by her greeting, Gain replied, "Who was I with? I was with no one! Why aren't you giving me a chance to explain myself before you accuse me of doing something wrong?" Still upset, Selena said, "You could have at least gotten rid of the smell before you tried to play me for a fool!" "What are you talking about?" Gain said in a moderately loud voice. He too was becoming upset. But Selena couldn't believe what she was hearing, so being fed up with the whole conversation, she yelled, "White Diamonds, you ninny! Why do I smell White Diamonds?" The door was still open during the shout fest, so Gain, realizing what Selena was talking about, calmed himself and said, "Selena, I'm sorry. I'll explain if you will let me. Can I please come in?" Selena lowered her voice as well, but she was still upset, so turning her back, walking away from the door, she mumbled, "Yeah, sure, you can come in."

Selena walked into the living room and sat on the couch. Gain followed and sat beside her at a distance. "Selena," Gain said, "I know what this looks like, but I have never been a person who lies. You can believe me fully when I say that I was not out having a good time with another woman. The perfume you smell came from a middle-aged woman's car. She just brought me back into town." Gain paused for a moment and lowered his head in frustration. Lifting up again, he lay back on the couch with his head in the air and his eyes closed. Then he said, "Selena, I was kidnapped."

"What!" said Selena, as she turned quickly toward Gain and gave him her undivided attention. She did not quite know how to take him because he didn't look at all as though he had been put in any danger. So she waited for him to say more. As Gain continued to talk, he opened his eyes and sat up saying, "What I'm about to tell you is going to sound strange, but this is actually what happened."

Gain went on to explain to Selena every detail of his past three or so hours. Selena responded by saying, "Gain, I have to admit, almost every single part of me wants to say you are lying, because nothing of what you are saying makes any sense. Gain, I drove by where your car was supposedly left, and I saw nothing. But you're right, as long as I've know you, never once have I called you a liar. You've never lied to me before, so why would you start now?" Gain had a confused look on his face because Selena said the car was not there. He finally said, "Wait a minute, you didn't see the car? It was exactly right where I left it, with the keys and my phone still in it. Are you sure you went down the right road?" "Wilson Street, right?" asked Selena. Gain nodded his head yes. "And the time was about six thirty," added Selena. This was becoming too much for Gain to handle, so he put his hands to his head and said, "You know what, this is all getting a little too creepy for me. I do not know what is going on. I'm almost starting to believe that I imagined the whole thing." Gain got up from the couch, mustered up a smile, and said, "I know one thing that I am not imagining." Selena asked, "What's that?" Gain bent down, took Selena by the hands, and said, "My love for you." Selena smiled as her heart began to feel Gain's heart. "Give me a call tomorrow," she said. "Maybe we can try to do something else this weekend." "Thank you," said Gain. "It hurts me so much to think of what you went through today. I just have to be more careful. I'll give you a call when I get home." "I'll definitely appreciate it," said Selena, as she walked him to the door and told him good night.

Though Friday evening was horrible for both Gain and Selena, patching things up between one another really helped them to get good-night sleeps. Gain knew that he could not let Friday's occurrence go without some investigation, but he also knew that he had to give Selena a wonderful weekend. So he decided that he would deal with the other issue on Monday. Besides, he had practically no idea of what was going on.

So on Saturday, around noon, he gave Selena a call. He knew how much Selena loved go-kart racing; therefore, he asked her if she was in the mood for a few laps around the track. Of course, Selena said yes, so Gain picked her up at two, and they headed out to have some fun together. Once again, Team One heard Selena and Gain's plans and made their own plans to mess things up between them. When Gain and Selena made it to the track, the lines were not too long, so they decided to race once before they got something to eat. After their first race, they went inside to order some food. While standing in line, Selena noticed a nice-looking young lady staring at Gain as if she knew him. Gain didn't really notice because he was too interested in Selena. At the moment, Selena and Gain had a seat at their table, the woman, having the smell of White Diamonds perfume on her clothing, walked over, looking directly at Gain. "Hi, Gain," she said in a seductive voice, "why have you been ignoring me today? Last night was too incredible to get out of my mind.

Selena, darling, he likes you a lot, but he loves me. Didn't you get the hint yesterday?" As she walked away, she ran her fingers through his hair and said, "See you soon." While the woman was at the table, Gain attempted to say something but was too much in shock. He was nearly paralyzed. Selena was speechless and crushed, so she took her drink and splashed it in Gain's face. She then got up and said, "Do not ever talk to me again, do you hear me? *You big liar!*" Then she got up from the table and called Jacquelyn to pick her up, leaving Gain at the table wondering what is going on with his life.

For the first time since being a little boy, Gain cried. He didn't care about the drink all over his face, neither did he care that people were staring at him. All he could think about was that the one person, whose heart taught his how to beat, was gone. While he sat there, he tried to think of a reason to go on living without Selena but could find none. Gain didn't notice that Selena was just a few yards away on the outside of the building. She too was crying. Occasionally, she would look into the window to see if the woman was going to return, but all she saw was an obviously broken-hearted Gain, sitting alone. It made her cry even more. "Selena," Jacquelyn called. Selena turned to see that Jacquelyn had arrived, but she was too hurt to get up. So Jacquelyn sat down beside her on the bench and hugged her tightly for a few minutes before saying anything. Feeling Selena's pain, Jacquelyn also began to cry. Then she wiped her tears while still hugging Selena, and as she began to look around, she noticed that they were drawing attention. So she slowly let go of Selena, looked at her, and said, "Selena, let's get out of here. We'll talk in the car.

Okay?" Selena wiped her tears and said, "Okay." *That was their job. Team Two was to kill Gain.*

Team One had done their job, and a few members from Team Two were already stationed in the go-kart track parking lot. About an hour after Selena and Jacquelyn left, Gain decided to get up and go home. While walking to his car, he heard voices yelling as if there was an argument at the other end of the parking lot. He was too depressed to even look in that direction. Suddenly, a car started speeding down the aisle as Gain was crossing over from one side of that aisle to the other. The man speeding down the aisle was yelling at a woman who was in the aisle chasing the car and yelling at him. He was not paying attention to who was in front of him. Gain continued to walk, having no regard for his surroundings.

The car was about two feet from hitting Gain, when all of a sudden, he was yanked out of the way from behind. One of the workers there, who had been keeping an eye on Gain just to make sure he would be okay, was following him to his car and was there just in time to save Gain's life. "What are you doing, man??" yelled the worker. "Are you trying to kill yourself??" Gain realized what had happened and quickly said thanks, jumped off the ground, and ran to his car. "What's wrong with you, Gain?" he said to himself. He sat and thought for a while in his car before he finally drove home for the evening. He was still totally depressed, but he figured that somehow, someone, for some reason, was out to destroy his life. However, instead of trying to figure out who was trying to do it and why, as he said he would do, Gain decided to be safe and stay home for a while before going back out into the world.

On Monday morning, Gain called in to his job and said he would be out for the week. His boss was fine with it because he had become used to Gain's periodic absence during the times when he was on assignment with the League Elite. As the week progressed, Gain started to become fearful of going anywhere other than home. This was strange because Gain had never been afraid like this. He was not getting better; he was actually falling deeper into depression. Although he felt safe at home, being in the house all the time was making him sort of lose his mind. He was also starting to get a bit claustrophobic. Therefore, he decided to go out into his backyard and get some fresh air.

He had no idea what he was in for. Team Two was upset that Gain was still alive. They were not going to let him get away on the next encounter.

He had only his pajamas on and a t-shirt when he walked outside. As soon as he had gotten near the end of his backyard, he heard the sound of growling dogs. Team Two had let loose three dogs, which they had injected with rabies. When the dogs saw Gain, they immediately rushed after him. Gain noticed the dogs running after him, so he attempted to run away from them. It didn't happen. One of the dogs caught hold of Gain's pajamas and caused him to trip. The dog pounced on top of Gain and tried to bite him in the neck. Gain, with all his strength, wrestled the attacking dog in order to stay alive.

As the struggle continued, Gain and the dog started to roll, because at the point where Gain fell, his backyard sloped thirty yards down to a stream. The two other dogs noticed the slope and turned to run in a different way. Meanwhile,

Gain and the other dog had begun to roll very fast down the hill, until finally, they both splashed into the water. Instantly, the dog let go of Gain and ran away. The water was shallow, so Gain kept himself in the stream for a while before he got up. His arms and legs were scratched and bruised, but he was okay. Amazingly, the dog did not bite him once. Gain did not want to go back to his house. In fact, he started to wish that he had let the dog kill him. He was afraid to go anywhere and wasn't sure as to what his next few seconds entailed. He thought that if he stayed in the stream, somehow piranhas would show up and eat him. On the other hand, if he moved from his present spot, something even worse might happen.

After about two minutes, he saw what he believed to be a water moccasin swimming toward him. Gain jumped out of the water and started running barefoot and dripping wet up the hill, past his house, and down the street to a neighborhood Catholic church. He did not know what else to do, so he frantically knocked on the door, hoping that someone would answer, and someone did. The man who came to the door introduced himself as the priest of the church. He told Gain that he would be in for an hour or two. Instead of saying his name was Father So-and-so, he simply called himself Melvin. As he invited Gain inside, he asked him what had happened. Relieved but still confused about what was going on in his life, Gain asked the priest if he would lock the door and take him somewhere private to talk. Knowing for certain that Gain was desperate, the priest locked the door and took Gain into an office. "Thank you, sir," Gain said softly. "That's why I'm here," the priest replied. "Now how can I be of service to you—" "Gain," interjected Gain, "my name is

Gain, and the way you can help me is by listening to my story and telling me"—Gain's voice got a little louder—"what... is going ... on!" Gain's voice did rise a bit, but he was in no way disrespectful to the priest. The priest responded to Gain's request by saying, "You can start whenever and wherever you like. I'm listening."

Over the next hour and a half, without interruption, Gain gave the priest a condensed but detailed story of his life: from the time his father died up until the moment he knocked on the church door. The priest thought intently about Gain's story because in many ways, it hardly seemed believable. Nevertheless, he knew deep down that Gain was telling the absolute truth about everything. The priest responded to Gain's story saying, "Wow! You've been through all of that, and you're still alive, sitting right in front of me in one piece. Can I get your autograph?" Gain laughed a little and began to relax. The priest continued, "Let's first deal with the issue of whether or not someone is after you. The answer is yes. If everything you've told me is true, you are a wanted man right now, and you are being followed. Be careful when you get ready to leave out of here."

Gain knew that what the priest was saying was true, but he was sort of hoping it was all just a bad dream. Therefore, he sighed after the priest stated his opinion. The priest sensed his dismay and said, "But I really believe that you are going to be okay." "I hope so," said Gain. "The important thing," said the priest, "is not to let your very own fears be the cause of your death. You have to stay sharp." "Now," continued the priest, "the answer to what is going on in your personal life is quite clear to me. I didn't hear anything about religion or

God as you shared your story, so I hope I'm correct in saying that you are not too familiar with how spirituality works in a person's life." "Yes," said Gain, "you are absolutely correct. I've never been one who attended church regularly." Gain paused for a second or two and asked, "That's not going to be an issue, is it?" The priest said no and that he was excited to share with Gain the best solution for his problem.

"In the Bible," said the priest, "there is a very commonly used quote that comes from a very wise spiritual leader of the Christian movement. His name was the Apostle Paul. I'm sure you are going to be quite intrigued after you hear it. It goes, 'For to me, to live is Christ, and to die is gain.' Pretty weird, huh? You had no idea that your name was connected to such a popular quote from the Bible of all places." Gain began to scratch his head and think back to whether there was ever a time his mom or dad told him the reason for his strange name. Perhaps, too much had happened in his life for that discussion to ever arise, he thought. Nonetheless, he was quite intrigued, just as the priest had said.

The priest continued, "Gain, what the Apostle Paul meant by that statement was that he believed in this person call Jesus Christ so much that all of his life would be devoted to telling others about the message *he* left. And that, because Jesus's message was that there was everlasting life for those who believed in *him*, 'dying' in the Apostle Paul's eyes meant that things would get even better than his life on earth. "I know this may be a little confusing, and I assure you that I am not trying to convert you to Christianity. That choice, you will make *if* and *when* you decide. However, I am now going to tell you how that quote applies to your very own life. Deal?" Gain smiled and said, "Deal." The priest asked Gain this question, "Before you became truly romantically involved with Selena, what was your attitude toward death? Were you ever afraid of dying?" Gain, knowing exactly what he was like, said right away, "Oh, that's an easy one. Sir, I honestly cannot remember a time when I was ever afraid of dying. I just didn't really have to think about it. It's like I kinda knew how to avoid trouble and get out of bad situations. The thought of death…there was no way I was going to let myself die." The priest then said, "When you say, 'let yourself die,' it sounds as if you felt responsible for your fate, whether you would live or die. So let me ask you this. Is it safe to say that your feelings about failure were the same as your feelings about death, that is, there was no way you were going to let yourself fail?"

The room was quiet for thirty seconds or so, then Gain said, "Now that I think about it, you may be right. I remember, even as a little kid, always feeling as though people depended on me. I just could not let them down. So yeah, failure was not an option either." "You know what I believe, Gain?" said the priest. "I believe during those times in your life, prior to falling in love with Selena, if a situation arose where you would have had to choose death in order to succeed, with no questions asked, automatically you would have chosen death." With a puzzled look on his face, Gain said, "Huh? How is it possible for me to have succeeded if I had died?" "Listen, Gain," said the priest. "Every time you did something dangerous, it was for a good reason. So as your life progressed, you had grown accustomed to suppressing that natural fear of dying so much that it had become buried deep in your subconscious. Therefore, whenever you had to face death but escaped it, there was no recounting of the details or analyzing what may have happened if. In your mind, you believed 100 percent that the cause was greater than the consequence. In other words, dying to save someone or make things better in the world to you would have been worth it."

As Gain listened, he was beginning to understand more about himself, but there was more to learn, so the priest continued, "Now that there has been a huge change in your life for the better." The priest smiled. Gain smiled as well because he knew the priest was speaking of Selena. "Your love for Selena has brought about a problem with your ideology. You, my friend, are now afraid to die." Gain lowered his head. And as he lifted it up slowly and sighed, he said, "You're right, I am afraid to die." The priest said, "I think I know why, but can you put words to what I'm thinking?" Gain said, "I think so." The priest said, "Go ahead." Tears began to fall from Gain's eyes as he started to think about Selena. He said, "No one, not even my mother, has ever meant as much to me as she does." He chuckled a bit while still crying and said, "It's not even close. Selena equals the world to me. When you said that at one point, the cause was greater than the consequence, well, if the cause forces me to lose Selena, then I want no parts of it. You cannot imagine how much pain I am in right now. I may never get her back."

Unable to speak anymore, Gain started to cry even more almost uncontrollably. At that point, the priest got up from his chair and walked around his desk to where Gain was seated. He then knelt down and, placing his hand on Gain's shoulder, began to console him. The priest said, "Gain, you know this could be the beginning of the best days of your life because everything has surfaced now. Nothing is suppressed. All we have to do now is talk about how you can walk out of that door, confident that better days are ahead. Let's give it a shot." Gain dried his eyes and said, "Okay." The priest stood up, sat on his desk, and said, "If you find a cause that is greater than the consequence of losing Selena, then you will be able to escape death, or live a full life despite your fears. You feared losing Selena. She's already gone. So why not make it your purpose or cause to expose whoever did this to you and make things right again? I really believe that all you need, Gain, is a reason to want to live. This can be your reason. What do you think? Is this something you can work with?"

By now, the look on Gain's face was one of a person who had just heard some good news. No longer was he feeling as though there was no hope. Thus, when the priest asked him if his idea was one he could work with, Gain stood up smiling and said, "The only reason I came knocking at your door was to hide. I was scared out of my mind and nearly, if not completely, suicidal. It is incomprehensible to me how this one encounter with you has made me feel as though I can literally conquer the whole world by myself, if need be. So yes, taking on the task of making things right again is something I can and want to do. I only have one question before I leave out the door. Who are you, really?" The priest replied, "It is not me who is about to face the challenge of a lifetime, but you. Who I am is not important, but it is more critical than ever that you never forget who you are." With those final words, the priest escorted Gain to the door. On the way out, Gain noticed a card on a table near the door, with the church's information on it. He asked the priest if he could have it just in case he needed some more advice. The priest said, "Sure." "Thank you," said Gain. "You're welcome," said the priest, and Gain walked out the door headed home.

No one from Team Two expected Gain to have lived, and they did not want to be around when the dogs started attacking Gain; others hearing might have gotten suspicious and called the police. Therefore, they all left the scene as soon as they saw the dogs chase after Gain. Also, Gain's wallet was still in his house. So for the first time in a while, no one knew Gain's location. When Gain walked inside his house, he went over to his wallet to put the card away. As he began to slide the card into one of its pockets, he noticed that it wouldn't fully slide in. He took the card out, turned the wallet upside down, and began to shake the wallet so that whatever was in the pocket would fall out. Right away, the tracking device fell out onto the floor. Gain reached down and picked it up. Realizing what it was, he sat it on the table and disguised his voice saying, in a loud whisper, "Come on, man! Hurry up! Just take the whole wallet. Stop lookin' in it!" He changed his voice to a softer tone, but louder than a whisper, "Wait! Something fell out! Somebody might be listening to us." Back to the other voice, he said, "Well, smash it, and let's get out of here!" He then took a pair of pliers from the drawer and broke the device.

Listening to what they believed to be a burglary, Team Two was even more convinced that Gain was no longer alive. They immediately informed Mr. Wilde of the news. Meanwhile, Gain knew that the device came from the League Elite headquarters, so he took the broken pieces of the device and put them inside a plastic bag and kept it. He very much wanted to call Selena and let her know what was going on, but he figured it best to get more information first. So he gathered a few things that he would need for a week away from the house. Then he packed them into a bag and began his walk to rent a car. He did not know whether or not his car was bugged, so he left it home as well. He also changed his cell phone number and told no one the new number, except his parents.

Patching Things Up

At the beginning of that same week, Lance and Mr. Wilde met to discuss how the team would get everything set and ready for the Drug Hound. Although they were in agreement at the meeting with the secretary of Homeland Security, Lance had one problem with Mr. Wilde's choice to wait until all of the canisters were in place before activation. He figured that it would be best to start activation in the major cities, which would allow people to recognize its effectiveness and easily join the crusade. He said, "Mr. Wilde, I do understand the symbolism behind your method, but I believe that if we wait too long, other groups may arise and say we should not do it. We may very well lose the support, and the plan will be scrapped." In a raised voice, Mr. Wilde responded, "How is it that we've gotten this far and done this well through my leadership, and now you feel you know what's best? Who's been making the decisions thus far?" Lance lowered his head and said, "You have, sir." Mr. Wilde continued, "Well then, let's not make any changes to the way we operate. Is that understood!?" "Yes, I'm sorry I ever brought it up," said Lance.

Mr. Wilde had communicated clearly that the main purpose is unity and that this was an opportunity for the country to come together and do something big. However, the reason he wanted to wait was because he knew that once the contaminated canisters were activated, many would die quickly, and the process would be halted immediately. The only way he could rid the country of the greatest amount of addicts was if he waited until all canisters were in place. Mr. Wilde was determined to see that day come. As Lance and Mr. Wilde continued to discuss the plan, they determined that it was time to have another League Elite meeting so that everyone would be on board and aware of what was going to happen in the near future.

The meeting was held on the evening of Gain's talk with the priest. Mr. Wilde told the league members that Gain had a few personal issues to deal with and that he had chosen to take some time off and go away for a while. He said, "Although we would really love to have Gain here with us, this plan doesn't call for any major heroics, so we'll be fine. Let's just keep him in our thoughts. I'm sure he'll be back in no time."

He told everybody that their major jobs would be to inform as many people about what the Drug Hound does in order to take away their fears of something going wrong. He gave them each a huge booklet about the Drug Hound. In one week, they were all to read and understand the entire book and be able to give a full presentation to anyone who asks about it. He said, "We want this country to be safe and at the same time feel safe. This is why it is crucial that each of you take the time to become well informed of this new invention. Oh, and before we leave, let's give Greg and Lance a hand for their hard work and dedication to this dream I've had since before most of you were even in grade school." Everybody clapped for Lance and Greg, and when they were finished, they left the building.

As they were leaving, Mr. Wilde pulled Selena and Lance to the side and told them that he wanted them to work together on a special project. He told them that they were to create a marketing slogan and gimmick that would represent what LIFE Academy, Life League, and League Elite are all about, past, present, and future, with the Drug Hound as the main feature. This was Mr. Wilde's way of giving Lance the opportunity to get to know Selena better. Selena was still a little sad about Gain; the news of his departure made it even worse. So she told Lance that she would get with him on the weekend.

By now, Mr. Wilde had already gone, so Lance, noticing that Selena looked a little down about something, asked her if she would like to go get a bite to eat. Selena didn't really want to go but figured that there was no harm in going; besides, she hadn't eaten breakfast yet. "It'll be on me," said Lance. Selena smiled and replied, "Oh, that's nice, Lance, it really is, but I'm fine. I'll pay for myself." Lance really wanted the honor of treating Selena but did not want to seem pushy, so he agreed. They made the decision to meet each other at the restaurant about two miles from Selena's house.

While they were eating, Selena said, "Lance, do you find me attractive?" Lance was not expecting that question at all, but he had always found Selena attractive, even when they where at the academy. So he answered, "Yes, I do find you attractive, very attractive, in fact—" Before Lance could say another word, Selena interjected, "Well, why is it that Gain doesn't find me attractive? I mean, he's told me before that I'm a beautiful woman and that no one has made him feel the way I do. Is Gain a liar? Did he just say those things to make me like him more? I thought he was the man I would one day marry, but noo..."

Selena did not stop talking about Gain, and every time Lance tried to answer what he thought was a question, she would start up again before he could begin the formation of a word. This went on for at least forty-five minutes straight. Occasionally, others close by would take a quick look at Lance and pity him because the expression on his face said it all, "I'm trapped, please help me." Finally, Lance gained enough courage to signal the waiter for the check. When Selena saw this, she said, "Oh, is it time to go already?" She looked down at her watch and said, "Wow, it's amazing how time just flies by when you're letting off steam." Lance said nothing. He was afraid that if he tried, she would start talking again. When the waiter came with the check, they put their money together, plus a tip, and left the restaurant. Lance remained quiet until he reached the door handle of his car, at which point he finally said, "I'll see you around, Selena." Selena smiled and replied, "Yeah, thanks for talking to me." Lance got into his car and drove off, a bit frustrated to say the least. As Selena watched him drive off, she started laughing. Then she got into her car and drove home.

Anxious to talk to Jacquelyn, Selena rushed into her house and picked up the phone to dial. "Hello," said Jacquelyn. "Hey, Jackie," said Selena, "do you have a little time to talk?" "Sure," said Jacquelyn, "what's up?" "Well," said Selena, "About an hour and a half ago, Lance asked me to go and get some breakfast with him, so I told him yes." Jacquelyn was surprised that Selena went with him; therefore, she asked, "So you're interested in Lance?" "Not even a little bit," said Selena, "I only went because I did not want him to bother me anymore, and after this breakfast, it will be awhile before he thinks of asking me out." Jacquelyn asked, "What did you do?" Selena answered, "Nothing, except talk about Gain the whole time." They both started laughing as Selena continued, "I don't think he said a word after I started talking. It was sooo fun. Although, I did feel a little sorry for him, because he is a nice guy."

They continued to have a few more laughs, but then Jacquelyn asked, "So how are you holding up? It sounds like you're at least feeling better." Selena answered, "Well, that's also part of the reason I called. While I was purposely trying to irritate Lance, I actually started thinking about Gain. I know I'm not over him, and I'm not sure if I want to be." "What do you mean?" asked Jacquelyn. "I'm thinking that when he does come back, I'll give him another chance. We have too much history together, and I don't believe either one of us really gave the relationship a chance to grow."

In the meantime, Gain was still in a hotel room, a few miles from his house. The night prior was the best sleep he'd had in a week or so. He was up, alert, and ready to figure out who was after him and why. His only hesitation about going out was the uncertainty of knowing whether or not he was still being followed. So he made sure that he was careful with every move he made. Every five minutes, however, he would think about Selena, so it became extremely difficult to effectively calculate and process his next move. Finally, he decided that he would call her and leave a message on her answering machine. He did not know she would be home.

When Gain called using the hotel phone, Selena could not recognize the number, so she decided to let the answering machine pick it up. When prompted to leave a message, Gain said, "Hi, Selena, this is Gain. I know that you said for me to never talk to you again, but honestly, I do not think my life was meant to exist with out you in it. I do not know how I'm going to convince you that I've done nothing wrong at all, but one day I will. Anyway, I could not get you out of my mind, so I thought this might—" Just then, Selena, who was moved by what Gain was saying to her, said, "Hello." When Gain heard her voice, he said nothing for about ten seconds. At first he thought he was imagining her voice, but Selena said, "Hello? Gain, are you still there?" Gain responded, "Oh! I'm sorry. I wasn't expecting you to be home." Selena was a little nervous, but Gain didn't notice because he was quite nervous himself. "Wow, the retreat must really be working, huh," asked Selena. "What retreat? I haven't gone anywhere," said Gain. Selena answered, "We had a meeting this morning, and Mr. Wilde told us that you were going away for a little while because you had to deal with a few personal issues?" Rather than trying to defend himself and risk losing touch with Selena, Gain said, "Selena, I know we haven't spoken to one another in about a week, and our last conversation was the worst we've ever had, but can you meet with me so we can talk? That's all I ask."

Selena was upset at Gain because she just couldn't believe that he lied to Mr. Wilde, so in a mildly raised voice, she said, "Is that how it goes? You do whatever you want and lie to whomever you want, and you think that's supposed to be okay with me? I don't think so, Gain. I need an answer to why you told Mr. Wilde that you were going away if you had no intentions of going anywhere? Are you trying to keep something secret?" Gain responded, "Selena, I know you're not enjoying this conversation, but I believe we'll talk better if we meet at the park. Is that all right?" as she calmed down, Selena said, "That's fine, I'll meet you there in about twenty minutes." Gain said, "Okay—Oh, Selena! I almost forgot to tell you to look for a gray-haired overweight man with a mustache, wearing a pair of black slacks and a baby blue shirt. That will be me, in one of my new disguises." Selena wanted to laugh, but she didn't. She simply said, "I'll be there," as they hung up the phones. Gain got himself ready and took the plastic bag containing the broken tracking device.

When they met at the park, they both said, "Hello." Then Gain continued to talk, saying, "I did not lie to Mr. Wilde about going away. In fact, I cannot remember the last time he and I had an actual conversation. I guess I've found the person who put this"—Gain handed Selena the plastic bag containing the device—"in my wallet. I just, for the life of me, cannot figure out how he did it." Selena was in shock. At first she did not want to believe Mr. Wilde would do such a thing, but then she thought about how much this device would explain. She said, "If it is true that Mr. Wilde has been spying on you, then it is possible that all of the events that transpired last weekend were set up. But that also means that someone could still be after you." Gain said, "Just before I called you, I was also thinking that someone was still after me and that it wasn't safe for me to go anywhere. But what if whoever was after me thinks that I'm dead?" Selena asked, "But why would they think that you're already dead? Didn't you break this tracking device after you found it in your wallet?"

Gain answered, "Yes, but there were two instances where I was almost killed. The first happened after you left the go-kart track. Someone tried to run over me with a car. They would have succeeded had I not been pulled out of the way. Then yesterday in my own backyard, I was attacked by three huge dogs. Selena, I was so afraid. I thought I was going to die that very moment. The only thing that saved me was that the dog and I rolled down that slope in my backyard into the stream." Selena, who had her hands covering her mouth the whole time she listened, said, "Oh my goodness, Gain. You mean, someone tried to kill you *twice*?" Gain replied, "Yes, but I seriously believe that the worst is not over." Selena paused for a moment and thought about how she accused Gain of being so many things that he never was. Then she continued, "Gain, I am so sorry that I believed Mr. Wilde over you. He's the one who says and does what he wants. This time, however, he said a bit too much."

"Actually," said Gain, "it's a good thing he said it because at least now we know it's him who's after me. The hard part is finding out why." "So," said Gain, "what was the meeting about? Does the league finally have a new mission?" Selena smirked and said, "We have a new mission all right, but it involves doing something that none of us are really wired to do." "What's that?" asked Gain. "Marketing," answered Selena. "Our job is to create an excitement in this nation about the Drug Hound. Also, by next week, we must all have read and understood the operator's manual for the Drug

Hound. Other than that, Mr. Wilde paired Lance and me together for a special project. We'll start on it this weekend."

"Selena," asked Gain, "what's the vibe like among the members when it comes to the Drug Hound?" Selena responded, "Oh, everyone is extremely excited about what it will do in our country. Lance and Greg have really outdone themselves on this one! Why do you ask?" Gain simply shrugged his shoulders. Then Selena said, "Gain, please don't tell me that you have a bad feeling about this invention. It took so long for us to get it FDA approved, and now it's received full support from the necessary individuals in government." "Okay," said Gain, chuckling, "I won't tell you." "Gain, this is not funny," said Selena, "You can be so…so… how is it going to be when we—" "When we what?" asked Gain. Selena sighed and said, "Never mind."

Selena and Gain went on to talk for another two hours. They really did love each other, but during their conversation, they made an agreement that until they solve this case, they would not take the relationship beyond friendship. They wanted to focus all of their efforts on figuring out why Mr. Wilde wanted Gain dead.

Just before they parted ways, Gain thought back to his time with the priest. He remembered how sure the priest was that things were going to get better. He could not understand how only a day had passed and things were already much better. He asked, "Selena, why is it that you and I have never become churchgoers? I mean, we're good people who always try to do the right thing, so if going to church is a good thing, why haven't we done it?" Selena responded, "Well, I used to go sometimes when I was in the orphanage, but I didn't really like it, because every time I prayed for something, it seemed like it never happened. I don't know if I've ever honestly believed in God and Jesus and all that stuff." Gain said, "Wow, me either. I do not remember ever believing in God like the people who go to church do." Selena was curious, so she asked, "Why are you talking about this? Have all the close calls with death brought you more in touch with your spiritual side?" "I will tell you this," said Gain. "There is a huge difference between how I viewed life yesterday and all the days prior and how I view life at this very moment. Why don't I just come over to your house some time this week, and we'll talk about it." "That will be okay…I guess?" said Selena. Then they both said good-bye and left the park.

The next morning had come, and Mr. Wilde was meeting with the leaders of Teams One and Two in his home. He was beginning to wonder why there had been no reports of a young man found dead. "It's been almost two days now, and I haven't seen or heard anything! Are you certain you took care of Gain?" The leader of Team Two said, "I saw the dogs attack him, and there was no reason for me to believe that he would escape the grasps of these crazy dogs. Maybe they dragged him somewhere." "That may be so," said Mr. Wilde, "but if I do not here anything by tomorrow morning, we're going to have to assume he's still alive, and if he's still alive, that's not good for me."

Morning came, and Mr. Wilde still had not heard anything concerning Gain. He was, however, fully aware of Gain's relationship with Selena. Therefore, he decided to have Team Two follow Selena. They did not want her to suspect anything, so they used multiple cars to keep tab on her.

Mr. Wilde knew that if Gain was alive, he would no doubt find a way to keep in contact with Selena. This time, the orders given were, "If you find him, kill him by any means necessary. I do not want him around anymore! And once he's dead, do not worry about the girl. I'll deal with her myself."

Not the Same Gain

On Saturday morning, Selena gave Lance a call in reference to their project. They decided to meet at the league headquarters at around ten o'clock. When they arrived, it was all business. Lance had already drawn up some ideas for posters, and Selena had a few catchy phrases like Cocaine Is Out, Clean Is In; Cocaine Is Not Fun, It's a Loaded Gun; and Beware Cocaine! The Drug Hound Will Sniff You Out! Lance and Selena were actually having a good time merging their ideas into one. Lance was enjoying himself so much that he loosened up a bit and started telling Selena what he wanted to tell her on their breakfast date. He said, "Selena, when we were having breakfast together, you asked me a question that I didn't get to fully answer. You asked me if I thought you were attractive." Selena started to get a little uncomfortable, so she tried to say something to stop him. She said, "Lance, I really don't—" but before she could finish her sentence, Lance said, "I know, I know, you really don't want to hear about how beautiful you are, because Gain doesn't make you feel that way. But what about me, Selena, I have to matter for something. I just think you are a little afraid to hear the truth about yourself. The truth, Selena, is that…" Just then, Lance started saying a poem that he had written for her a few years back, "You are cute and cuddly, pretty and prissy, tall and tingly too."

Selena could not take any more. She became woozy, nauseous, and irritated all at the same time. She put her hand over her mouth, held her stomach, and walked quickly, but carefully, outside to get some air. Lance, for some reason, did not know it was he who had made Selena feel this way, so he followed her outside and asked her what was the matter. Selena was starting to feel better, so rather than possibly having to hear more of Lance's poem, she said, "Lance, you are a very, very nice guy, but I do not think I will ever become interested in doing anything with you outside of work. We are strictly League Elite team members. I am sorry I had to tell it to you that way."

What Selena said to Lance crushed him so much that he forgot she was right in front of him. He started saying things out loud, like, "I don't even know why I listened to Mr. Wilde anyway. I knew she was out of my league. He says that he's the boss, and he knows what's best, but I don't think he's right—" "Right about what?" asked Selena. "Oh, you heard me talking?" asked Lance. "Yes, I did," said Selena. "You said you don't think Mr. Wilde is right about something. What is it that you don't think he's right about?" "It's nothing," said Lance, "nothing you should worry about. It's something the inventors have to worry about." Selena replied, "Lance, do you know how many horrible mistakes happen because people feel that they don't have to inform others of serious issues? Now, because I am a part of this team, it is your responsibility to let me know if something wrong is about to happen. Do not hold back on me, Lance. What's going on?"

Lance told Selena everything. He told her how he had always viewed Mr. Wilde as a second father and that he thought that all of his intentions were pure. He also told her what Mr. Wilde said about Gain being involved in illegal gun distribution in order to convince him to deactivate his alarm. Selena wanted to choke Lance, but she knew that he was tricked, so she continued to listen. "I would do anything for Mr. Wilde," said Lance, "up until a couple days ago when he basically told me that my opinion did not matter when it came to the plans for the Drug Hound. He was like a different man. I had never heard him speak to anyone like he spoke to me. I felt utterly disrespected."

Lance continued, "It was at that point that I started to think about all the things I had let him do to me in the past. I even thought about how he made me sign documents for him when I was too busy to look at them. Selena, I do not trust Mr. Wilde in what he wants to do with those canisters. So yesterday, I went into his office to look for the documents that I had signed, but all of his files were locked in the cabinet. What is he hiding from us and why is he blocking me from helping to make sure that everything works out as best as possible?" Selena responded, "It's obvious that he's trying to shift responsibility on you." "Yeah, I can see that clearly now, he's setting me up. I only wish I had seen it back then. Still, I've got to get to those files."

Selena was anxious to get back and provide Gain with this new information, so she and Lance decided to conclude their meeting with the understanding that Lance would get hold of the documents as quickly as possible. When he gets the documents, he is to contact Selena, and they will meet. Selena then parted, leaving Lance at the headquarters. He said he wanted to sit and think for a while.

Selena did not know about the person tasked to follow her, but he was there. Since the league headquarters was located among other businesses, his car blended in with the others. Prior to leaving league headquarters, Selena had given Gain a call to let him know that she wanted to meet at her house. Gain agreed. He then traded in his rental car for a work van and put on a different wig and mustache and dressed himself as an electrician. The person following Selena drove past her house after she parked, leaving someone else from the team to keep watch over who would enter her home.

Selena had eaten lunch and had been home for an hour and a half before she heard a ring at the doorbell. She was not expecting anyone else, so she figured it was Gain. When she looked through the peephole, she didn't initially recognize him, but looking at his eyes and nose, she knew it was Gain. However, just to be sure, she asked, "Who is it?" Gain responded in a soft voice, "It's me, Gain." Then she let him in. Gain and Selena talked for about an hour, trying to figure out what Mr. Wilde's plan for the canisters could be. Neither one of them came up with anything; they needed Lance to get hold of those documents. *They did not have any plans yet. Are you saying that I should mention what they discussed even though it was not helpful?*

One week had passed, and Selena, Lance, and Gain were in the same position as before: clueless as to what Mr. Wilde was doing. Just as well, Mr. Wilde's team of followers was in the same position as before: clueless as to where Gain was hiding. It was like a game of hide-and-seek. Gain and his crew were trying to find what Mr. Wilde had hidden, while Mr. Wilde and his crew were trying to find out where Gain was hiding. Progress with the Drug Hound was moving along swiftly and enthusiastically. It seemed as if the entire nation was on board with the project. Therefore, it appeared that all the canisters would be in place within two more weeks. Mr. Wilde started getting nervous and angry that the team had not yet found Gain.

Gain had amassed numerous disguises. He managed somehow to never look the same. He had also spent a lot of money on his disguises and was almost out of money because he had stopped going to work. At the same time, he was starting to get clingier to Selena. Selena was concerned that he was becoming obsessed both over her as well as with hiding and disguising himself. In Selena's eyes, he just was not the same Gain.

Not only was Gain obsessed, but so was Mr. Wilde. He knew that Gain was plotting something, and he started to think that some of the members were in on it. With that in mind, Mr. Wilde decided to close the league headquarters until activation day. He figured he no longer needed any of them. However, he still wanted Gain. So he told the team of followers to do what some of them wanted from the beginning: kidnap Selena and hold her hostage, and in no time, Gain would be in their hands.

On the very same day that Mr. Wilde had given Team Two the orders to kidnap Selena from her home, Gain received a phone call while Selena was still at work. It was on his cell phone, which he had changed after he went undercover. When the phone rang, he said, "Hello." "Hi, Gain, it's your uncle Phil." "Uncle Phil!" said Gain. "Did my mom give you my number?" "Yes, she did," said Phil. "Oh well, I guess some things aren't meant to be kept secret." Notwithstanding, he was so glad to hear his uncle's voice. Gain hadn't spoken to him for about a year but felt a sense of peace for a moment, but then he became cautious because his uncle was an active Life League member. Gain had developed distrust for anyone associated with LIFE Academy, except for Selena. Nevertheless, he and his uncle continued to talk. "Gain," said Phil, "I'm sorry I haven't called you until now. And I really cannot say that it's because I was busy. So let me make it up to you by taking you out to lunch." Gain agreed, so he put on another disguise and met his uncle at a restaurant thirty minutes later.

Phil did not know where Gain was until Gain tapped him on the shoulder and said, "Uncle Phil, are you ready to eat?" Phil almost flipped when he saw Gain in a disguise. "What is this, Gain?" he asked. Gain told him that he would explain later as the two took their seats in a booth. Phil was a little uncomfortable talking to his nephew in a disguise, but he ignored it. He started the conversation by saying, "When we were on the phone, the reason I said I was not thinking of you much is because I thought everything was fine. I'm not so sure now. Gain, what's going on with you?" "What do you mean, Uncle Phil?" asked Gain. "Everything is going fine with me." His uncle answered, "Well, I've kind of heard some things like you haven't been to work in three weeks. You've left the League Elite. You are running and hiding from something. And there is no need for me to go on, because you sitting in front of me in a silly disguise is proof enough!"

Gain responded very directly, "Yes, I've been on the run, so to speak, but it's for a very good reason, and I'm not sure if I can let you know why." "Look, Gain," said Phil, "whether or not you want to let me in on your secret is totally up to you. I will not make you tell me something that you wish to keep from me. However, I will say this. You are no longer Gain Lampley. You have become someone else." Immediately, Gain's mind was taken back to what the priest told him: that he should never forget who he is.

As his uncle continued to talk, Gain realized that he had lapsed once again into living in fear. Then he looked at himself and his disguise, and piece by piece, he began to unveil himself, until at last, the true Gain sat, exposed, unafraid. "Well, that's much better!" said Phil. Gain smiled almost like a child who had made his parents proud. "Can you tell me now what or who has you afraid to be seen in public?" Gain responded, "To be honest, I think it has been me all along. But if you want to know what is going on in my life, I'll start by saying Mr. Wilde." Phil looked confused, "Mr. Wilde?" he said. "Has he done something to you, or have you done something to him?" Gain responded, "Oh, he has definitely done something to me, but I realize the real problem is not what he's doing to me, but what he's about to do to who knows how many."

Gain told his uncle about the times he was almost killed, about the tracking device, and about how he and Selena had been racking their brains trying to find out why Mr. Wilde was after Gain. He did not mention Lance because he was not certain if he should trust him. He told him that all of their effort had given them nothing. Phil listened to Gain but did not seem surprised. Phil was waiting to hear some incriminating news so that it would prove what he had been feeling about Mr. Wilde for years.

"Gain," said Phil, "you know that I've known Mr. Wilde for about thirty years now, and ever since I've known him, he's been an extremely smart, powerful, and influential man. None of that has changed to this day. If anything, he's even more influential because of the success he's had throughout those years. If you are trying to find out anything from him, he's going to have to tell it to you directly. No one will speak against him. In the past, he's gotten away with doing things that should not have been done, because, sadly, no one dared challenge him, not even me. However, because he knows so much and controls so much, he's also become very arrogant. That trait will be his eventual downfall."

Phil continued, "Your father was a very smart man as well. We both were. The only difference is that I was a LIFE Academy graduate, and he wasn't. Allen, for some reason, did not like Mr. Wilde. Perhaps it was because he blamed him for taking me out of his life for so long. I was three years older than your dad, and when I left, he was still in elementary school. Anyway, after Allen finished college, he began to do some research on Mr. Wilde and the LIFE Academy. A few years after he started his research, Allen came across some information and showed it to me. It revealed something that made me question Mr. Wilde's ethics. It had something to do with a homeless person. I can't quite remember it now, but I was shocked, so I went directly to Mr. Wilde and asked him about it. He told me that there are many things written about him that are complete rumors, totally untrue, and most of all, cannot be proven." Phil paused for a moment and began to tear up just a little. After a minute or so, he wiped his eyes and said in a trembling voice, "One week later was when Allen was killed." Gain stared straight ahead, thinking about that day, that moment when his father died. He felt as though the wind had been knocked out of him. Then he lowered his head and wept. For about two minutes, the table was silent, except for the faint sound of men crying.

Finally, Phil continued to talk, though Gain's head was still lowered. He said, "Gain, I've been in this organization for all these years, waiting for something to surface about that incident, and nothing has. I've been waiting for Mr. Wilde's antics to be brought to a halt, but they never have. The only reason I told Mr. Wilde about you and your gift was because I knew that one day, you would be the one to expose him." Phil touched Gain on his shoulder, and Gain lifted his head, wiping his eyes. "Gain, now is not the time to run. This is your moment to do part of what you were brought into this world to do. The rabid dogs are no coincidence. I know now for sure that Mr. Wilde killed my brother, your father. It's time for the world to know what we know. He is not a hero. He's a murderer, a man who will stop at no point to get what he wants, even if it requires the spilling of innocent blood." "Only you can do this, Gain," said Phil. "You have to meet him face-to-face." Gain responded, "I'll do it. I have a cause now that is greater than the consequence." Phil said, "So you're ready to be you now?" Gain answered, "I'm ready."

Phil then told Gain that all he had to do was meet Mr. Wilde in a public area and talk to him about his father.

"Eventually," said Phil, "he will say something wrong, but you have to push his buttons, get him upset that you have the audacity to confront him. You'll be wired with a clear cordless monitor that brushes into your hair with one brush and out of your hair with the other. We will be able to pick up on the entire conversation. You'll do well. Are you okay?" "I'm fine," said Gain. Gain told his uncle that he would like to meet with Mr. Wilde as soon as possible. So they agreed that if Mr. Wilde obliged, the meeting would be held the next day around noon. After they had finished eating, Gain went with his uncle to get the monitor.

The whole time Gain and Phil were talking at the restaurant, Amy of the League Elite intelligence division, was listening in another booth. Her back was toward Phil's back. It was just by happenstance that she was there. She did not hear everything, but she heard them speaking negatively of Mr. Wilde, and she heard that they were going to try and set him up. So while Gain and Phil were getting things together for the meeting with Mr. Wilde, Amy was informing Mr. Wilde of their plan.

A Cause Greater than the Consequence

The news Amy brought to Mr. Wilde was a very pleasant surprise. The man he'd been chasing for weeks had decided to meet with him face-to-face. As it pertained to Phil, Mr. Wilde chose to give him a call and invite him out to his home. Not wanting to arouse any suspicion, Phil accepted Mr. Wilde's invitation and went out to Mr. Wilde's home. When Phil walked in the door, two men grabbed him, tied him up, and sat him down at Mr. Wilde's table. When Mr. Wilde walked into the room, he said, "I only have one question for you. If you knew I was so, in your words, smart, powerful, and influential, then why would you even think of bringing me down, let alone concoct a full-fledged plan to incriminate me?" Just as Phil opened his mouth to say something, Mr. Wilde yelled, "You are not allowed to speak!" Then calming down a bit, Mr. Wilde continued, "All those years of receiving the highest of accolades, we've accomplished so much, yet you give it all up because you think I'm going to admit to something I did not do. One thing's for certain, your brother was the smarter one.

You utterly disgust me! The Life League will deal with you appropriately." Mr. Wilde then told the men to cover Phil's mouth with tape and put him in the basement closet.

About thirty minutes after Phil had been placed in the basement, Mr. Wilde received a call from Gain. He acted as though he knew nothing of the plan. After they exchanged greetings, Mr. Wilde said, "Gain, it's so good to hear from you. How have you been, my friend?" Gain responded, "I've had better days, but I'm okay." "Tell me," said Mr. Wilde, "what is the nature of your call?" Gain replied, "I would like to have lunch with you tomorrow around noon to discuss a few things with you. Is that possible?" "I'm going to be busy all day tomorrow, until around five o'clock," said Mr. Wilde, "but if you'd like, we can meet in my home at six. After tomorrow, I'll be booked for the next two weeks." Gain knew right away that saying yes meant walking into danger, but he also knew that he could not wait two weeks. Too much could happen by then. So he agreed to meet Mr. Wilde at his residence at the appointed time. When they ended the conversation, Mr. Wilde called to make sure that everything was in order for Selena's kidnapping. His plan was to display Phil and Selena before Gain's eyes just before he had him taken out and executed. Watching Gain's expression as he watched helplessly his loved ones suffer was going to be a form of sweet revenge for Mr. Wilde. No one had ever put him through as much agony as Gain.

Hanging up the phone, Gain called Selena. She had just walked out of the office and was about to head home. Since he had been so clingy over the past week or so, Selena did not really want to talk to him. Nevertheless, she answered the call. She told Gain that she would prefer if he would call back after seven o'clock. However, because Gain knew he wasn't guaranteed much more time with Selena, he insisted that they have another talk at the park. Selena sighed and said, "Okay, we can meet today. It's just that I'm a little tired." "No problem," said Gain, "I promise not to keep you out long." Still unenthused, Selena said, "What disguise should I look for this time?" Gain replied, "Just look for a young man who looks exactly like the man who loves you more than anyone on earth." Selena perked up and said, "So no more disguises?" "I like me better," said Gain.

As Selena drove to the park, no one followed her because the mission had changed, and there were people at her house waiting to kidnap her at gunpoint so she wouldn't make a scene. Selena, however, would never go home.

During their talk at the park, Gain told Selena what was about to happen and how necessary it was for him to go through with it. Selena understood, but told him that the only way he could do it was if they develop a plan that included her in it. It pained him so much, but Gain said yes to Selena's involvement, and they put their heads together to make a plan.

When Gain and Selena parted ways for the evening, Gain went to the neighborhood church where he spoke with the priest. He figured that there was a chance that the priest would be there. When he knocked on the door, someone came to the door, but it wasn't the priest. Gain said, "Wow, I really didn't expect for anyone to be here this late." The person asked, "Then why did you knock?" Gain chuckled and said, "Well, it's just that a few weeks ago there was a priest here who helped me so much. And I kind of wanted to tell him thanks." The person at the door started scratching his head and said, "Priest? There hasn't been a priest here in about a year, in fact, we did not reopen until a week ago. You must have the wrong place of worship, sorry." Then the man closed the door.

Gain wanted to say more but did not know what to say. He took out the card in his wallet, and it matched exactly the name on the building. Gain did not know what he should do. He did not know whether to be afraid or if he should feel special or what. So he did what people always do when they believe they've experienced the presence of God. He knelt down at the church steps and prayed. He said, "God, I'm very new at this, but I do want to say something to you. You have made me believe that you are real, so here it goes. I am scared of what is going to happen tomorrow. If I am not supposed to meet with Mr. Wilde, then can you let me know? I know you can, because you made that priest talk to me when I had no one. If you say nothing to me, I'm going to meet with him. I just hope that you make a miracle happen. Okay, God." Gain went to his own house that night and slept in peace.

Part of the plan was that since Mr. Wilde still trusted Lance and thus he maintained the privilege of entering the league headquarters, Selena would convince him to get into the building and shut off all alarms, which would allow them to break into his office and dismantle the file cabinet and retrieve every document signed by Lance. The process took them five hours to complete. They knew that at any point Mr. Wilde could come in, so they made sure that they got out by three in the morning. They went through all of the documents by twelve thirty and kept all that they needed, putting everything else back into the file cabinet after Selena had reassembled it. Gain rearmed the building, and they left one hour after the documents were retrieved.

Lance and Selena knew that they had a big day ahead of them, so after leaving the headquarters, rather than driving sleepily back to their homes, they slept in two rooms at a hotel nearby. They woke up at eight o'clock the next morning and started going through the documents as fast as possible. Out of all the documents, most of the documents were legitimate, but there were ten different documents, which spanned five years, that were written in a different language. Neither Lance nor Selena knew how to interpret the documents, but they knew Jacquelyn could. Lance and Selena had already called in to take the day off, but Jacquelyn was at work.

By now, it was ten thirty, so Selena called her, but she was out of the office and would not be in until two o'clock. Lance and Selena could do nothing but wait. All Gain, Lance, and Selena had was a very strong notion that something illegal was going on with Mr. Wilde, and they each felt that the proof would be found on the documents from the file cabinet. The plan was that Gain would have received and copied the incriminating information from Lance and Selena prior to the meeting. Having received it, he would threaten to go public and expose Mr. Wilde if he did not reveal what he was hiding. That was all they had, nothing else. Gain had asked God for a miracle, and that's what it would take for this plan to bring down Mr. Wilde.

That same day, around ten in the morning, Mr. Wilde had a meeting with Amy and a few members of team two about trying to locate Selena. He was sure that the two were plotting something against him, and he told them that they both needed to be stopped. He took Amy into his office and told her that she would be given a high position in the Life League if she were able to locate them. Amy was an extremely ambitious person, who, one day, wanted Mr. Wilde's position. She knew that this would be perfect for her. So she accepted his offer. As she prepared to leave, she noticed Mr. Wilde's file cabinet. She said, "Mr. Wilde, your file cabinet looks sort of weird at the top. Has it been broken before?" Mr. Wilde looked at the file cabinet, took out his keys, and opened it. He looked for those documents and found none of them. He became enraged. "Lance!" he said, "Lance is in on it too! I want them all *dead*. Nobody steals from me…I mean *nobody!*"

At that moment, they began to look at the alarm system, and the in and out log. They found that Lance had tampered with the system and that they left the building early that morning. Because they left the building at that time, there was a chance that they checked into one of the hotels. Therefore, she left swiftly all alone to see if what she thought was correct. When she got to the hotel, she saw Selena's car, and gave Mr. Wilde a call to come and get them.

At the precise time that Amy pulled into the parking lot, Selena was looking out of the window as they waited for two o'clock to call Jacquelyn. She saw Amy hovering around her car, then she saw her get on the phone. Immediately, she said, "Lance, we got to go! I think someone is on to us. Amy is downstairs hanging around my car. We're going to have to go in the same car. Since it's only Amy, she will not try to stop us, but we will definitely have company following us when we leave. When they got downstairs, Amy confronted Selena and said, "There's no use in running, you may as well give up." Selena replied, "How about, I choose to ignore you and try my best not to hurt you. Now get out of my way!" Amy stepped out of the way and allowed them both to enter the car and leave.

Amy had placed a homing device on the car, so Mr. Wilde and his crew would know their every move. When Selena had driven about three miles from the hotel, they noticed cars following them. Selena looked over at Lance and said, "She tagged us." Lance replied, "I figured she would. And we have no time to stop and look for it." "That's okay," said Selena. "Do you have your car keys?" "Yes, I do," said Lance. Selena continued, "Here's what we're going to do. We'll let them keep up with us for a few more miles. Since this is single-lane traffic, and there is a good bit of cars out here, they won't be foolish enough to try anything. They're just trying to keep us moving until we run out of gas, but that's not going to happen." "And what are we going to do again?" asked Lance. "You'll find out," replied Selena.

At about the tenth mile from the hotel, Selena was driving about sixty miles per hour, when suddenly, she made a sharp right turn and drifted into the opposite direction. Within seconds, she was speeding in the direction of the hotel on the side of the road. When she saw there was a break in traffic, she sped into the appropriate lane and headed back to the hotel. It took Mr. Wilde's crew about five minutes before they could get themselves together and begin to follow her. By that time, Lance and Selena were almost to the hotel. When they reached, they abandoned Selena's car, gathered everything into Lance's car, and drove to another hotel, where they waited until they could call Jacquelyn at two.

While Lance and Selena were out dodging Mr. Wilde and his crew, Gain was content with staying in his house. He had not been there in so long that he did not want to go anywhere else. Gain also took the opportunity to call and talk to his mom for a little while. It was almost as if he were taking time to enjoy the small things in life. He knew that there was a high probability that this was his last day of life. Nevertheless, he was ready.

At around two thirty, Mr. Wilde went back to his home to prepare for the meeting with Gain. He had already decided that there would be no meeting. His plan was that as soon as Gain stepped into the house, he would be grabbed just like his uncle. Only there would be no talking. He would simply show Gain his bound uncle and then have him executed immediately after. Mr. Wilde wanted Gain's last moment of life to be one of complete hopelessness. He had never really liked Gain; he only wanted to use him.

Meanwhile, Selena and Lance had completely lost Mr. Wilde's crew, including Amy, who had begun to yell at everyone around her. For Lance and Selena, this was perfect, because even after they had gotten in touch with Jacquelyn, she said she couldn't make it to the hotel until around four o'clock. They told her to hurry, but she did not arrive until five minutes after four. When she walked into the room, they gave her the documents to translate. They were written in ancient Greek, a language that was somewhat familiar to Jacquelyn, but there was a great deal of words to translate. The good news was that they found on four different forms all of the information about the canisters and how they were contaminated for the purpose of making America a better place. Every form cited Lance as the person responsible for the contamination and that he deemed it an absolute but necessary evil. Lance was floored, and Jacquelyn and Selena could not believe they were a part of his organization.

The bad news was that by the time all the forms were translated, it was fifteen minutes before six o'clock. They knew that there was no longer a need for Gain to even meet with Mr. Wilde, because they had everything they needed to stop the process. So they tried to contact him, but they could not. He had already left for the meeting and chose to leave his cell phone home, because he did not want Mr. Wilde to take it from him and be able to contact and harm any of his loved ones. The hotel was about twenty-five minutes from Mr. Wilde's house because of the traffic, but all Lance, Selena, and Jacquelyn knew to do was try to get there as fast as they could.

On the way there, Gain had to make a stop because he saw a little boy struggling to fix his bicycle. So Gain, figuring he had enough time, stopped his car, got out, and helped the little boy to fix his bike. "That was fun," said Gain to himself. He drove for about five more minutes, and he had to stop again because he saw a woman trying to change her tire. He just could not fight the feeling to help her. When he offered to help, she said, "Please, because I have no clue as to what I am doing." This job took up a little bit more of Gain's time, but he still figured he'd only be a few minutes late. Then when he was only a three blocks away from Mr. Wilde's gated and guarded home, he saw a man trying to push his car up a small incline and into the gas station. For some reason, Gain felt compelled to help this man, even though it would for sure make him at least ten minutes late. For some reason though, when Gain started to help push the car, it was heavier than he imagined, but he toughed it out. When they finally got the car pushed to the pump, it was already ten minutes after six. Gain was sweating and late; both made him nervous to walk into the meeting with Mr. Wilde.

When six o'clock came and Gain was not at his door, Mr. Wilde became angry that Gain would be so disrespectful to him. At five minutes after six, Mr. Wilde started to get so mad that he wanted Gain dead at the door. But at ten minutes after six, Mr. Wilde sent men out to the gate to grab Gain as soon as he took one step out of his car. Then they were to take him to the backyard for execution. He had become so angry at Gain's downright insolence that he did not even want him on his doorstep.

At twelve minutes after six o'clock, Gain pulled up to the gate guard, who lifted the wooden bar for Gain to enter. Gain parked his car about ten yards away from the gate, and just as was planned, when Gain stepped out of the car, three men rushed in to grab him, but he was so fast they could not lay a hand on him. Then they took out their guns to shoot at him, but before they could, Selena rammed Lance's car through the bar and drove directly at the men with guns. As they jumped out of the way, Gain jumped into the passenger seat window, and Selena, who was driving by herself, sped off with Gain unharmed.

Mr. Wilde knew his ship had sunk, so he jumped into his car and attempted to leave his complex, but just as he was about to leave, Lance and Jacquelyn showed up with the FBI. It was the biggest bust in United States history. If they had been notified a week later, one of the darkest days would have occurred in America at the hands of one man obsessed with his hatred for drugs and those who use them.

One week later, Gain, Selena, Lance, and Jacquelyn were honored as heroes. Together, they went on to start their own nonprofit organization to offer hope and opportunity for children in crisis. The entire LIFE Academy, Life League, and League Elite were placed under investigation and one-year probation. After Mr. Wilde was arrested, he ratted out everyone who followed him including Amy. Although they all were prosecuted, none of them received nearly as harsh of a penalty as Mr. Wilde, who was also convicted for the murder of Gain's father, receiving a total sentence of fifty years imprisonment. Phil, who was found bound in Mr. Wilde's dining room, made sure of that.

Three months after their organization was established, Jacquelyn and Lance made the announcement of their engagement. Gain and Selena had not quite made it to that point, mainly because Gain was really into church, but Selena was not. Nevertheless, they were as close as ever. A funny thing happened that same month. A man, seemingly in his middle to late twenties, walked into the center, asking to speak to Selena. Lance, who had first addressed the man, said, "Sorry to tell you this, my friend, but she's madly in love with someone right now." The man chuckled and said, "Well, that's good news to me, but can I speak to her and at least get a chance to congratulate her on her successful relationship?" Lance said, "Sure, I'll get her."

When Selena walked out, she almost fainted, but the man caught her. He looked her directly in her eyes and said, "You've become a beautiful woman." She responded in a soft voice, saying, "Alvy, it can't be you! I thought I would never see you again." Alvy then said, as he lifted her up and sat her on a chair, "You may never have seen me if you guys would not have found out what that Wilde guy was doing." Selena said, "What do you mean?" "Selena," said Alvy, "the reason you haven't seen me in all these years was not because I couldn't get to you. My adoptive parents always wanted me to go visit you, but I had become too preoccupied with doing the wrong things and doing bad things in gangs. I couldn't face you, knowing that I was your older brother and was supposed to be an example of how to live right."

Alvy continued, "Well, eventually I ended up in jail for taking the blame for something I didn't do. I learned my lesson when I was in there, but when I came out, I couldn't find a decent job to support myself. Three years of struggling brought me to my lowest point, so I decided that I was going to turn to drugs to kind of escape it all. I remember it vividly, and I probably always will. I had just purchased my first bag of cocaine and was watching TV, getting ready to try it for the first time. Just when I leaned down to snort, a news flash popped up of the arrest of that guy and what his intentions were. I pushed myself back as far as I could from that cocaine and never touched it again. That was a turning point for me, and I just wanted to tell you guys personally that I thank you for saving my life."

Alvy hung around for a few hours and even helped out a bit. He met Gain, and they both agreed that they would keep in close touch. He also had lots of fun with Selena, talking about the times in the orphanage. After he left, Selena had a talk with Gain. She asked, "Do you remember asking me about God and all that stuff?" "Yes, I remember," said Gain. "Well," said Selena, "I remember telling you that I did not believe in God and Jesus and all that stuff, because he never answered my prayers. Well, I have to change my position on God answering prayers. The one prayer I would always pray was that I would one day reunite with my brother. I do not know why my prayer wasn't answered until now, but I do know that the way it was answered made me feel that it was well worth the wait." Gain smiled and asked, "So what are you saying?" Selena replied, "I'm saying that I do believe that God answers prayers. The rest…well, I'll agree to learn more about religion and faith, as long as you're patient with me. I promise I will not take too long.

A year later, Selena, Gain, Jacquelyn, and Lance had a double wedding in the church that Gain said saved his life.

www.ingramcontent.com/pod-product-compliance
Lightning Source LLC
Chambersburg PA
CBHW060402080526
44583CB00012B/431